"UNRECOGNIZED"

"Unrecognized" Pt 2

Bad Blood, Cliques, & The Federal Government

Edited by Simone J. Smith

Graphic Design, Artwork, & Authorship

By Guy Smith

After the French dubbed the lands the Ozarks, long before the U.S. government built the plethora of man-made lakes within the area of the plateau in the 1900s, the Native American peoples that called these lands home were linked throughout the area by the rivers and waterways & thus created new cultures in the process.

This Work is Dedicated to:

My Ancestors who decided to call the Ozarks their home, to all the disenfranchised Indigenous peoples that can be found across the United States of America, and to the educators who wish to learn more about Native American issues, both past and present. It is also for people who wish to challenge the narratives and stigmas held toward Native communities of the past. This book was written for those who seek to understand the history of the Nations, Tribes, Bands, and Families of select Indigenous groups, and it is also for the benefit of those that want to broaden their understanding of the Ozarks by peering at its past through a different lens.

Preface

To whom it may concern,

I write this to give you a brief overview of issues that Native groups in the Ozarks region of the United States face. The breadth of available knowledge and literature pertaining to Native groups in the Ozarks is extremely limited as it stands today. As a result, there are many prejudices and misconceptions held by both natives and non-natives alike; one of which assumes that affiliated tribal members are solely motivated by monetary gain. While this narrative is a popular one, this notion could not be further from the truth. Many Indigenous groups in the Ozarks have maintained their heritage for hundreds of years. I hope that this work can help to move us away from old labels based off bad policies, such as "full bloods" and other racially driven terms based on blood quantum, and restructure how we view Native American identity today within the United States.

Best regards,

Kyle "Guy" Smith
Independent Ethnographer & U.S. Combat Veteran
Myrtle Beach, South Carolina, United States of America

Acknowledgments

I would first and foremost like to say thank you to my wife Simone because without her this work would have never come into existence. She put the idea in my head that I could do this and supported me in it every step of the way. She drove me around the country and helped me in the countless hours of research. Some of the most pivotal discoveries came on account of books she bought for me thinking that I would find them relevant to my work. Simone does not know how much she has done for me in this endeavor, and not to mention all the things that she helps me with daily, as it has put me forever in her debt. I would also like to acknowledge my children; I want them to understand their heritage and to know that it is important even though others may act like it is not. Andre, Kash, and Maxine, I love you all and hope you appreciate this in your later years once I am gone. I would also like to thank my mother, Pauletta Hollister, I miss her daily, as well as my grandparents, Maxine and Richard Hough, and my Aunt Carole- may she Rest in Peace as well. You all were, and always have been there for me. I could never thank you enough for raising me to be the man that I am today.

I would like to thank Dr. Jim Sullivan of MiraCosta College in Oceanside, California. His support for my work did not go unnoticed. Dr. Sullivan showed me that while someone may not know your perspective that does not mean that they are unwilling to look at the alternative views that you may hold. Some of the papers I wrote for him would become my starting point for the research for this book. I would also like to give thanks to Folklorist Dr. Rachel Gholson for her guidance on how to go about tackling certain aspects of this work. Lastly, but by no means least, I would like to thank Dr. Richard Carlson as his impact cannot be understated. I cannot thank him enough for the personal guidance that he has given me and for his contributions as an ethno-historian who has dedicated his life to researching the Indigenous peoples that we hail from. To everyone else in my life, I appreciate you all as well, even if you are not personally mentioned by name.

Introduction

In the last volume of this book, we covered the history of the Ozarks, Native American Identity, and a myriad of other facets that came about because of racism and Jim Crow in the past regarding the indigenous peoples of the North American continent. One should know now what many issues arise for the various Inter Displaced Peoples that exist within America in terms of historical documentation and having to explain the diasporas of their peoples. In this volume we will look at how these many movements have cause bad blood and tensions in various ways and how this has not only affected how we view history, but how it has had a great effect on the groups that have been muted in their lives.

This book looks at multiple states of tribal affairs in modern times, weighing them against their historical context, and pries apart the facts from the historical gas lighting to get a full understanding of the plight of "unrecognized" communities in Indian Country today. By the end of this work the reader will have a full understanding of how the past can be skewed. This is done threw reinforcing an echo chamber of Ethnocentric views, recounting selective documents, events, and family groups as holding the "official claim to histories", all to benefit the interests of certain political factions of a tribe, such as shown with the Cherokee Nation within these pages. I hope this work inspires others to strive to document the full histories of tribes. Everyone has equal rights to live on this earth and have their story represented.

Table of Contents

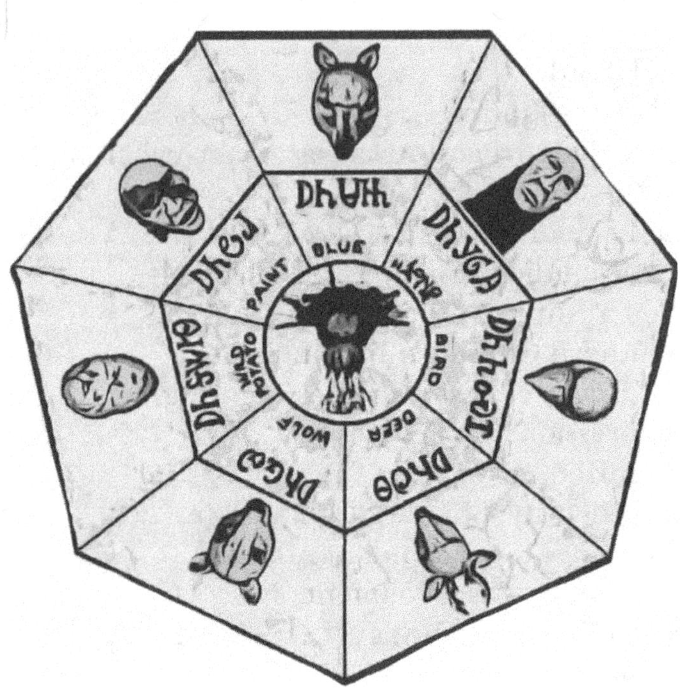

*"The earth is the mother of all people, and all people
should have equal rights upon it."
- Chief Joseph*

THE SAD TRUTH

The issues of Native American peoples in the United States come up low on the radar of the federal government. The issue that has been created of "unrecognized" peoples and the inherently murky waters that are the power politics played by the now "recognized" tribes at the expense of Indigenous groups as a result, have come out of racism-based politics in Indian Country from the civil rights movement until now by federally aligned groups. This is no better displayed than looking at the long held ties the biggest Indigenous nation in the land has to the federal government. Looking into the Cherokee Nation's complex history, one that since the American Civil War has become even more convoluted as the times have gone on, we can see how money and power influence the actions of some of these federally recognized groups. As one of the first "Civilized" tribes the members of the Cherokee Nation have been exploited by its elites and the officials of the United States government since the creation of the Cherokee government of Old in 1794. From first contact, through the Removals, during the Reconstruction Era, Jim Crow, and through the Civil Rights Movement, much of that history has been deliberately skewed to fit the narrative of the Cherokee Nation of Oklahoma, now just the Cherokee Nation, who since the start of their tribal body, has tried to claim to be the authority on Cherokee history even though they are but just one faction of the larger group.

Many factors lead to why the Cherokee Nation has become the antagonist to smaller Cherokee factions, none more so however than that they are motivated by political power, monetary gains, and the control they have as the gate keepers to aid from the federal government. This has become the state of the Nation for the Cherokee peoples now; however, one of the most important factors driving the divisions in the past was, and still is, the sovereignty and political identities of the individual factions. In this article I will go over a summary of how the Cherokee Nation has performed cover ups, currently performed historical gas lighting, and used intimidation to achieve its goals, and how it continues the exclusion and discrimination of other Cherokee factions in the process. Continuing to advocate to keep them un-recognized and thus out of the fold of the federal tribal registry and the benefits and support that are entitled to all Indigenous peoples through trust doctrine through it.

CHEROKEE IN-FIGHTING

The story of the Cherokee peoples in the southern Appalachian Mountains started around 8,000 BC. The Cherokee were among one of the largest and most powerful Indigenous confederacies occupying around 140,000 square miles in what became parts of North and South Carolina, Tennessee, Alabama, and Georgia. As you can see the Cherokee Nation of Old was once a sprawling expansion of land. As such, each town was governed by its own set of peace and war chiefs, and while the towns were linked through culture and commerce, there was in no way a centralization of governmental power for the Cherokee Nation in the beginning, such as there was with other tribes like the Iroquois Confederation with their "Longhouse" meetings of united tribal Chiefs.

The Cherokee were freethinkers. People/individuals who had vision beyond the present. Making their decisions with the future in mind, always acting for seven generations ahead with every choice they made, as to insure the best outcome for the world and their kin. They could reason beyond their emotion and were willing to sacrifice themselves for the future good of their people. This allowed the towns to keep the peace within the territory as the cultural beliefs and practices, such as the Cherokee law of blood, aka the Cherokee blood law, which is based on the idea that clan members could avenge the deaths or other incidents happening to their kin, being a matriarchal society woman often made the decisions about how those deaths were to be avenged, and this helped to keep the peace within the Nation. After decades of raids and attempts to protect themselves from excursions on them, Cherokee started to assimilate to western ways, leading them to gain the title of a "Civilized Tribe." However, Cherokees, post 1810, were seeing the writing on the wall and started to take a very real stand against the loss of lands to the immigrating Europeans into their country. With many becoming very capable capitalist, and engaging in matters of politics, the Cherokee elites decided to try to find compromise through the courts, in response to the flash point that was the series of laws passed by the Georgia state government to strip the local Cherokee Indians of their rights after gold was found on their lands. In court battles the Cherokee won in the landmark cases Cherokee Nation v. Georgia and Worcester v. Georgia, even though the rulings would not be followed.

In 1831 the United States Supreme Court sided in favor of the Cherokees first against Georgia upholding Indigenous rights and establishing the grounds for what would become the bases of government-to-government relationships and indigenous sovereignty as the Supreme Court does not hold the ability to enforce the rights of Native American "nations" against the states as it would be an overuse of power. Regarding the Cherokee Nation of Old, the Supreme Court ruled that it lacked jurisdiction to oversee the claims of an Indian nation within the United States as they are Sovereign to the Government itself. The Highest Court in the land made it clear that they were sympathetic to the situation Indigenous nations faced. Understanding that they had been persecuted and marginalized by the settlers but acknowledged that they have no power as they are both "foreign nations" and people within U.S. boundaries. However, in the year that followed, in the case, Worcester v. Georgia 1832, the Court also determined that only the United States Federal Government, and not the individual states, had power to regulate or deal with the Indian nations, and thus the Cherokees had all rights to their lands until ceded by Treaty between nations in a government-to-government agreement.

Regardless of the gains in the Federal courts, then President, Andrew Jackson, once a man who had a strong military alliance with the Cherokee Nation of Old in the recent past, decided to ignore the Supreme Court's rulings, and started to let Georgia enact their illegal laws without having to answer to his Department of Justice. This reunited old fires that had been smoldering over the decades of factional deep divides within the Cherokee Nation of Old, with most settling into two political camps, being the Ridge supporters, aka the Treaty Party, and the Ross supporters, known as the National Party. The Ridge group felt that the reality of their situation was that the only way for the Cherokee Nation to survive was to move west of the Mississippi, to Indian Territory, reuniting with the Cherokee who were already established in what was the Arkansas Territory then, a Tribe known as the Western Cherokees, or Old Settlers. They theorized if they did so they would be able to negotiate a relocation on their terms as they could not avoid the inevitable removal, as this was what the state of Georgia, the majority of the white land holders, and President Andrew Jackson desired. The National Party, or Ross group, however felt that it was the Cherokees right to stay in their lands and that they should fight to stay at all costs. The approach to make it happen was through continuous assimilation making the Cherokee Nation of Old's government in the eyes of the United States as much as possibly so. They theorized that if they continued to fight in the courts using the "white man's" laws to secure their spot they would ensure that Cherokee peoples would always have a place in what was then the Cherokee Nation of Old. Thus, the first Federally Recognized Band of the Cherokee Nation of Old was the Treaty Party. This faction is now known as the Southern Cherokee Indian Tribe today.

The creation of these groups escalated quickly, becoming gang-like and deadly, as under immense pressure the leaders of the Treaty Party prematurely signed the Treaty of New Echota on December 29, 1835, as there was not a full consensus among the tribal body before they did. With the famed Treaty Party leader Major Ridge stating after he signed, that he had signed his own death warrant, as he understood by Cherokee law that anyone giving away ancestral lands without full approval of the tribal government was to be put to death. This caused an immensely deadly schism between the two groups forever splitting the Cherokee Nation of Old for good. Soon after the Trail of Tears the assassinations began. Cherokee Law was enacted, and the Ross supporters started to murder the signers of the Treaty of 1835, their families, and any Ridge supporters and Old Settlers who would not concede to John Ross as the de facto Principal Chief of the Cherokee Nation in Indian Territory leading to a bloody civil war within the nation, and thus multiple exoduses out of Indian Territory of Cherokee factions into Missouri, Arkansas, Kansas, & Texas out of fear for their livelihoods.

At the beginning of the winter starting in the year of 1838, and ending in '39, the Cherokee peoples who did not remove already were forced from their homes in the lands that lay east of the Mississippi River, in the tragedy that was the Trail of Tears. Ill prepared, and with an overwhelming majority sick, in a piecemeal fashion Cherokees met up to make the journey to Indian Territory; believing that they still had a chance to repeal the treaty. While others fled to the surrounding hills to live on the less desirable lands away from white society, taking their chances as internally displaced peoples as a result. The Trail where they cried took many lives as the tribal factions who participated were forced under gunpoint by the U.S. Army to traverse across Tennessee, Arkansas, and the Southern parts of Kentucky and Missouri before ending their death march in Indian Territory. About one out of every four people died on the Trail of Tears. The cold and unrelentingly harsh winter led to a situation in which four thousand Cherokees died from hunger and disease, with thousands more lost to the winds due to fleeing into wilderness areas to avoid removals, and others that did it to escape the trail. The Cherokee Nation of Old in the East would be no more; forever fractured with bad blood and extreme hatred felt by the various Cherokee factions towards how the situation unfolded. After the removals, the United States went on to try to support the reestablishment of the Cherokee Nation to draw up a framework for the new homelands of the peoples in the northeast part of present-day Oklahoma.

Before the removals other factions of Cherokee had already made treaties with the U.S. and had established boundaries within what is now the state of Arkansas. These early migrants were known as the Old Settlers as previously covered and had already established a government upon the agreement of the Turkeytown Treaty of July 8, 1817, in which land in the east was exchanged for land in northwest Arkansas, north of the Arkansas River and south of the White River. Cherokee had already been in western Arkansas since as early as 1763, as the Cherokee who had allied themselves with the French during the Seven Years War, migrated west upon invitation at the end of the conflict because the French felt the Cherokee would act as a good buffer between their territory and places of commerce, such as Arkansas post, against the nations that held more hostilities against them such as the Osage. Some of the British allied Cherokee factions migrated west as well into the region that is now known as the Ozarks today after the British defeat during the American Revolutionary War. Another well documented third group migrated west from Tennessee in the early nineteenth century. These groups in what is now western Arkansas and northeast Oklahoma formed a large part of the Old Settlers, however there were other Cherokee Old Settler factions in places such as southeastern Kansas, Missouri, and Texas as well. These large migrations of full blood Cherokees were one of the reasons mixed bloods, such as the Ross and Ridge families, were able to gain such prominence and power in the Cherokee nation in the east, or the Cherokee Nation of Old, and subsequently help to sow the permanent divisions as they exist today.

The new Cherokees to the Territory after the forced removal in 1838 performed a coup d'etat on the Old Settlers. The newcomers to the Cherokee Nation West, as it was, immediately went about the plots to murder and coerce Treaty Party Cherokee to follow the will of the Ross faction. The Ross faction also wanted to establish a new government, and went about doing so, even though the Old Settlers already had one formed; this was brought about as the Ross group had full intentions on continuing slavery in Indian Territory to include the violent quelling of slave revolts and all.[1] While the Ridge faction members, such as Stand Watie and his family who were known Slave holders as well, allied themselves with the Old Settlers and had agreed to settle into their way of governance which would have meant no slavery, the Ross faction wanted the government based on that of the Southern white society where the power is in the courts of federal institutions and given to an elite political, economic, and racial driven class. This was in stark contrast to that of the Old Settlers governmental rule in where it was based more in old traditions through practices in which power for punishment and rule of the peoples was dictated by each individual town, led often by the Baptist convention of the group, and thus a localized action as discussed earlier, but in where education and religion were nation endeavors. The Ross faction however wanted slavery, and as such needed a Cherokee federalized government that would support that function and wanted to recreate the government structure that had been made in the Cherokee Nation of Old to achieve those ends. Thus, they went about the task of seizing power by waging a hot Civil War within the Cherokee People that started in 1839. Sadly, their Civil War one could argue is still active, although it changed from a hot war to a cold war in the 1930s and is still being waged in the courts today between multiple groups.

---

[1] Littlefield, Daniel F., and Lonnie E. Underhill. "Slave 'Revolt' in the Cherokee Nation, 1842." *American Indian Quarterly*, vol. 3, no. 2, University of Nebraska Press, 1977, pp. 121–31, https://doi.org/10.2307/1184177.

TRIBES IN MISSOURI AND ARKANSAS:

Inter-tribalism Within the Ozarks

The loss of status as recognized tribes in the 1800s was felt in full effect by Indian peoples in the years that followed the removal period, through The 1834 Nonintercourse Act that stated, " [N]o purchase, grant, lease, or other conveyance of land, or of any title or claim thereto, from any Indian nation or tribe of Indians, shall be of any validity in law or equity, unless the same be made by treaty or convention entered into pursuant the constitution".[2] Due to this legislation most tribes in the area made a move to practice their beliefs in private. Starting in the Alien Era and then moving forward into the Jim Crow period these people lived vary private lives in the hills. By doing so the Natives preserved their own distinct brands of heritage. Their perspective heritages then lived on self-sustained in what I refer to as unrecognized, self-established, Indian reserves.

These self-established Indian Reserves in the Ozarks were linked to the lands through private ownership that was acquired by intermixing with the Anglo families that came into their fold. Thus, the resulting mixed Anglo-Indian families would claim on paper to be "white" while still maintaining their own multicultural existence through cultural pluralism amongst their own, more full blood, Indigenous group. The inter-tribalism amongst the intermarried "minority whites," Whether they were French, German, or Irish, helped to bridge the gap between their full

---

[2] "25 U.S. Code § 177 - Purchases or Grants of Lands from Indians." *Legal Information Institute,* Legal Information Institute, www.law.cornell.edu/uscode/text/25/177.

blood Indigenous peoples and the white communities that surrounded their homesteads. To quote Kent Blansett on this subject, where he states in his paper, *intertribalism in the Ozarks, 1800–1865*, "Historians of the region have often explained the exchange of cultures typically as a one-way street, seeking to exploit a dichotomy between dominant and inferior, civilized, and uncivilized, savage, and exceptional, white and Indian. Yet the term exchange implies something much more complex. The Cherokee Nation did not become less Cherokee with the adaptation of printing presses, large scale agricultural production, and log cabins; in fact, it became something more. Even further, the Scots Irish who migrated into the Ozarks did not become less Scots Irish when they adopted native clothing, trade, and cultural customs. Each of these cultures became something greater; it transformed into an intertribal community by adapting to its region while simultaneously absorbing cultural traits or tools from other nations for its own political and cultural survival. Therefore, Ozarkians did not forsake their culture; they adopted intertribal perspectives that preserved and accentuated their own autonomy. "[3]

However, within many areas of the Missouri and Arkansas Ozarks, because of the native community's disbursement across small farmsteads and their relative seclusion in the hills, these tribal bodies also faced factors of racism and lack of economic resources among the Natives, as they only met in great numbers a few times a year. This use of land and space allowed the groups to stay out of the public eye to avoid removal from the land while still handling ceremony and tribal matters as family groups or bands the rest of the year through their churches.[4] Regardless, the Native American cultures continued to be passed on as they had for generations just with new stipulations to when one could

---

[3] Blansett, Kent. "Intertribalism in the Ozarks, 1800-1865." American Indian Quarterly 34, no. 4 (2010), 476.
[4] "Our People: Occaneechi Band of Saponi Nation." *YouTube*, 20 Aug. 2015, youtu.be/vkfNy-YJz_A.

practice their beliefs that adhered to the laws in place at the time. This is seen within the refugee Fort Christanna peoples as well as discussed by Martin Richardson when he writes about how the founders of the community that is now recognized as the Haliwa-Saponi, "maintained peoplehood by marrying almost exclusively among themselves, upholding cordial relations with whites, and keeping plots of land within the Native community." He goes on to say that this Saponi group in North Carolina, "utilized a number of economic and subsistence strategies, including hunting and gathering, as well as farming to meet their own needs." They also, "maintained a distinct Native community by adopting English forms of landownership, but local whites and government officials enforced white supremacy to threaten their legally owned lands."[5] This same process of acculturation to adapt to Anglo oppression by the American Indian communities happened in the Ozarks as well in where Anglo societies still ruled supreme over all forcing some of the Saponi into courts over the matter.[6]

Since the Native American communities could not win for losing by accepting the white concepts of land ownership and religion that was thrust upon them, in the late 1830s a healthy fear started to build up within the Native American communities towards both the state and federal governments because of the past actions taken against them and their relatives back East. This fear was based partly on past removals from their homelands, under promise of never having to remove again, the racial tensions of the Indians place within the states during the mid-1800s, as well as the possibility of future removals or death due to the laws on the books at the time, thus they put up a wall towards

---

[5] Richardson, Marvin M. "RACIAL CHOICES: THE EMERGENCE OF THE HALIWA-SAPONI INDIAN TRIBE, 1835-1971." *Carolina Digital Repository*, 26, 27. cdr.lib.unc.edu/indexablecontent/uuid:5211232d-556b-4793-82d3-e5a78baa8a17.
[6] "The Portuguese Connection ." *Documenting The Melungeons & Their Kin*, 23 Feb. 2015, the-melungeons.blogspot.com/2015/02/.

the outside surrounding communities of new incoming whites, that started in the 1840s and continued through the 1940s,[7] just as had been practiced back East prior to removing to the Ozarks as seen with the group that would become the Haliwa-Saponi peoples in North Carolina. To put the position of these groups into perspective, by this point at least three generations of Ozark Native Americans lived under racial scrutiny with the constant knowledge that if their heritage were found out, the best-case scenario for them would be that they would lose everything they had; while the worst-case scenario could mean that they would be met with their death. So in other words, the practice of reserving ones knowledge of their own cultural past to within the family had become a tradition by this point, and that tradition came with its own folk tales about past injustice and future wrong doings, that were reinforced by the communities ever present fears towards the government, making the lawman, or quite frankly any outsiders from their established safe families, the bogeymen, or more appropriately as their Boogers in real form,[8] ready to remove, or even kill, them like had happened in the early 1800s.

For an example of what life was like during the Jim Crow period for Native American communities in the Ozarks, we can look at Robert D. Cooter's writings titled *Individuals and Relatives*. In this paper Cooter interviews Robert Renfield about his childhood in a Cherokee Community in the Lapland area where Arkansas and Oklahoma meet. Cooter states that Renfield's recounting of his memories from his upbringing in the 1930s and 40s is a, "static account of the 'folk-urban continuum' into a dynamic theory of social development."[9] Renfield speaks

---

[7] Pavlik, Steve, and Robert K. Thomas. *A Good Cherokee, a Good Anthropologist: Papers in Honor of Robert K. Thomas.* (American Indian Studies Center, 1998), 70.

[8] Powers, William, "Returning to the Sacred: An Eliadean Interpretation of Speck's Account of the Cherokee Booger Dance," *The Journal of Religion and Theatre*, Vol 1, No 1, Fall 2002

[9] Pavlik, Steve, and Robert K. Thomas. *A Good Cherokee, a Good Anthropologist: Papers in Honor of Robert K. Thomas.* (American Indian Studies Center, 1998), 57.

to the Cherokees fear of outsiders when he states, "for instance, I remember my grandmother was particularly afraid of strange whites, and if one approached our house, especially if he were well dressed with fountain pens in his pocket, she would hide in the house and not answer the door. I was simply stunned silent by the appearance of strangers. Although my grandfather was a Cherokee to the very core in his attitude and outlook and was so in every way, he spoke several languages and had traveled all over the world, even though he had little formal education. He was a very sophisticated man, but most of the rest of us were simple, country people, 'fullbloods,' as whites will call us."[10]

Renfield also speaks to the fact that the home was a central location in where ceremonies for Ozark Cherokees took place. He goes on to say, "we had many religious ceremonies in our homes — birthright ceremonies, curing rights, funerals, purification of the house, herb medicine before eating 'green' corn, herb medicine at the Cherokee new year in October, hunting rituals at the fireplace, planting ceremonies at the garden, rituals to ensure plant growth at the garden in June, rituals to protect the house and garden from the fierce Oklahoma storms, religious purification at the spring before dawn many mornings, and so many more I can't remember them all. I also knew that my grandfather used the old Cherokee war medicine (prayers and charms) in his work as a constable."[11]

I would like to also state, just as a side note here, that within my peoples, the White River Band of the Chickamauga Cherokee, war medicine is still an important practice today; as I, while serving as a Civil Affairs Operator in Afghanistan, carried a small baggie in my right breast pocket filled with religious talismans, letters from loved ones, and tobacco, that I would pray over for strength and courage. My medicine is now a part of the U.S. Army's Chemical Corps Military History Collection and held at

---

[10] Ibid., 70.
[11] Ibid., 71.

the John B. Mahaffey Museum Complex at Fort Leonard Wood, Missouri. Other war traditions still continue as well such as the awarding of feathers collected by Elders for deeds done while in the service, as well as names earned in war, as they have been a practice in our culture for centuries as we believe you are given a name at your birth, but you also earn a name; and for us the way you earn a name is through service to your peoples. Such was the case with our great Chief Dragging Canoe as he got his name by trying to prove he was ready for the warpath as a young man by moving a canoe, however he could only drag it, and thus his name was born.[12] I myself was presented with a name by my tribe, however I do not readily share it with others, as well as feathers from an Elder, both of which were given to me post my time in combat. My peoples have a Warrior Society to which I am a part of with many more customs and practices. So much so that I honestly think a book could be written on that alone. However, that is not the point to this work so I will not indulge further, but I digress.

Back to the issue at hand, during the Jim Crow period the troubled relationships between Native Americans and the predominantly white communities around them made the task of opening up dialogue a challenge to do with the Federal government in the 1900s because many people still feared removal from their homes at the turn of the century and well up into the 1970s. United States policy in the early 1900s was to eliminate Indian reservations through allotments giving individual Indians land to own like any other person while selling off the rest of the land that the tribes had in common to the white communities around them. With the Indian policy of the time set on destroying the sovereignty of Indian Nations it is not hard to think

---

[12] "Dragging Canoe Was One of the Greatest Warriors of Cherokee Recorded History. A Cousin to Nancy Ward He Was One of the First to Propose a United Native Front against Westward Colonization." Tsi'yu-Gunsini - Dragging Canoe, Cherokee Chief, 1738 – March 1, 1792, https://www.aaanativearts.com/cherokee/dragging-canoe.htm.

that the tribal communities, even with their meager existence in Missouri and Arkansas, felt it was better to stay as unrecognized entities in contrast to the other nations around them that were losing their land hand over fist, and most importantly, their children to boarding schools for re-education.

In 1934, under the Indian Reorganization Act, tribes were given the ability to re-establish sovereignty and self-government. However, in Missouri and Arkansas the tribes were already self-sustaining without the federal government's involvement. This was because the government often tended to hurt more than it ever helped when it came to dealing with Native Americans by this point in American history. It should also be said though that the Native communities were hanging on to their way of lives by a thread at this point with the populations stretched thin, and with the extreme racism that was still in existence in the Jim Crow South, these groups felt it best to still stay isolated from the whole, rather than try to re-establish links with the Federal government or State governments, as racial violence was still common place. The idea that the tribes had to have government help to function was a lost notion to these Ozark Indians; toppled with the fears of removal the Missouri and Arkansas Indians did not see the point in raising an issue because they themselves sustain their land and culture internally viewing all others as outsiders. Also, a great deal of the peoples could still remember a time in the not too distant past when the words "I am Indian" could have had you removed from the state permanently, and as a result, many still believed that acknowledgment of their heritage would result in just that, the Removals of the families from the States.

The separation between the outside communities and the tribal bodies themselves stayed prevalent until more recent times. To add to this was the massive exodus of Indigenous peoples that took place due to the depression because of the lowering numbers of families who were able to keep their lands in the Ozarks. With a minor number of peoples still in the area just organized as smaller tribes, bands, clans, and even in some cases family groups, they continued their tribal connections through mass reunions that also acted as tribal meetings bringing the people from all over together again. This practice continued for most of the tribal peoples in the Ozarks well into the 1940s. Prior to this time, because of being from the lower tiers of society, there was by no means in which the tribes could legally reclaim their positions within the states of both Arkansas and Missouri as most people were not educated.

In our current times, as more laws are passed to protect the heritage and history of federally recognized tribes, these laws simultaneously adversely single unrecognized tribes out as non-authentic entities. This is because lack of documentation of these nations, such as the unrecognized tribal bodies in the Ozarks, as a result from the neglect of both the Federal and the State governments themselves, raise questions as to the authenticity of the tribes in the states of Arkansas and Missouri. As the tribes practiced on farmsteads away from any other governmental entities their presence was never officially recognized by the states and thus others claim that they have no history proving their links to their native tribes. As I have highlighted throughout this work, this is not true in the slightest; the tribes did not fully disappear, they continued during the end of the 19th and early 20th centuries and still have a presence today. While practicing in seclusion, during the Alien Era, the tribes left trails of their existence in mass culture through passages found in folklore publications, Newspapers, and personal writings spanning over the 80 years that Native Americans were barred from land ownership, or having the ability to hold citizenship, within the States of both Arkansas and Missouri.

Vance Randolph discusses the origins of Ozark culture, in his book Ozark superstitions, which was published in 1947, stating that, "Another view is that the hillman's superstitions are of Indian origins... The Pioneers did mingle freely with the Indians, and some of our best Ozark families boast of Cherokee blood."[13] Another account of Indians migrating into Arkansas

---

[13] Randolph, Vance. *Ozark Superstitions*. (Dover, 1964), 4.

is given by Hugh Massey, one of the former mayors of Mountain View, Arkansas, as he recalls Indian children who would play marbles on the school grounds with him in the 1910s. He said that the families would stay for two to three weeks before they would move off into the hills. He also stated that although many white men had tried to follow them, they were unsuccessful in their endeavors and the white people became convinced that they were mining for silver.[14] A more realistic view of how these Native groups used their space was that because they lived without legal representation, they had to adjust to a semi migratory life. A life in where these groups of families would have had to stay mobile, using various farms as safe houses, or secluded farmlands as squatter campgrounds, to avoid capture from state officials, the military, and para-military forces in fear of removal as was practiced in the past.

At the turn of the century, Vance Randolph talked of other Natives in the Ozarks, who still identified publicly as Indians even after the Alien Era was in full effect. He talks to the presence of multiple Cherokee traditional healers that one could still find thumping along in the White River region of the Ozarks during the days of his field work. An interesting figure he notes of was in the town of Hollister, as well as another Cherokee medicine man that could be found free floating around Taney County. He stated on the matter that, "People who visited Hollister, Missouri, in the spring of 1934 will not soon forget the 'prayin' corn doctor,' a bewhiskered old herbalist whose specialty was in corns and bunions and prayed loudly over his remedies. As late as 1940 there was one of these people in Taney County, Missouri, a long-haired chap with beaded moccasins and a deerskin vest. He carried many little bags of dried herbs, each marked with a mysterious sign supposed to be Cherokee picture writing." I find it interesting that Randolph

---

[14] Lankford, George E. "Shawnee Convergence: Immigrant Indians in the Ozarks." *The Arkansas Historical Quarterly*, vol. 58, no. 4, 1999, JSTOR, www.jstor.org/stable/40025509.

made a habit of speaking with other local Cherokees around the Ozarks, to include some groups that would later become included in the recognized Cherokee Nation of Oklahoma, to see the validity of the white communities' statements as seen when discussing fishing rituals. He states, "Country boys often leave one fish of a large catch hanging in a tree near the fishing hole. 'Oh, just for the birds,' a boy answered rather sheepishly when I asked him why this was done... A woman at Calico Rock, Arkansas, told me that it was a trick learned from the Cherokees, who always left several of their best fish lying on the bank. The old Cherokees whom I interviewed, however, said they never heard of any such foolishness."[15] While the presence of the medicine men speaks to their outright existence, the fishing traditions show how the customs differed between the Cherokee groups in the hills of Arkansas and Missouri versus the Cherokee groups that stayed within the Nation in Indian Territory that would later become the state of Oklahoma.

Another account of traditions that the Western Cherokee groups practiced in private in Missouri and Arkansas are those that require ceremonies with nudity and sex.[16] With traditions being brought from Tennessee, Kentucky, and Virginia. We know that Native Americans, were, and disproportionately still are, poor folk in these areas.[17] So knowing that fact the Native Americans are spoke of only in reference to their bathing practices as "low-class squatters" because all genders bathed together according to Randolph's writings. He goes on to make note that the respectable hill folk, I.E., people of Anglo decent, do not

---

[15] Randolph, Vance. *Ozark Superstitions.* (Dover, 1964), 103, 252.

[16] Randolph, Vance. "Nakedness in Ozark Folk Belief." *The Journal of American Folklore*, vol. 66, no. 262, 1953, 333. JSTOR, www.jstor.org/stable/536729.

[17] ZEDENO, MARIA-NIEVES, and ROBERT CHRISTOPHER BASALDU. "OZARK NATIONAL SCENIC RIVERWAYS, MISSOURI CULTURAL AFFILIATION STUDY FINAL REPORT." *DELAWARE TRIBE HISTORIC PRESERVATION OFFICE, 89..* dthpo.delawaretribe.org/wp-content/uploads/2012/01/OzarksCAS.pdf.

mixed bathe.[18] There is reference to a "wild clan" in southwest Missouri that used a magic ceremony involving nudity and chanting to produce a good harvest of turnips every year.[19] Randolph talks of an account of a family in the 1890s in which one of the daughters married a Cherokee. This family now practiced the Indigenous ceremony of running around their crops three times naked before then having sex upon the soil in the moonlight,[20] showing how not only were natives present during this time but also a force of influence within the surrounding communities of white settlers in their proximities by marrying within the families. There are a few more references to Native American rituals involving nudity however this covers it enough.

Randolph stated that he asked other Cherokees about sex rituals, and they said they had never heard of "such foolishness;"[21] keep in mind that, "Christianity had been established in the Cherokee Nation for decades prior to the removal. Beginning in about 1818 various denominations began sending in their missionaries to the Cherokee Nation. By the time of the first removal detachment in 1838, Native Christians numbered in the hundreds, perhaps thousands, including many Cherokee preachers and lay workers."[22] According to the official history the migration of Cherokee groups from the East to the Ozarks started in 1692.[23] With the peoples coming in contact with the

---

[18] Randolph, Vance. "Nakedness in Ozark Folk Belief." *The Journal of American Folklore,* vol. 66, no. 262, 1953, 333. JSTOR, www.jstor.org/stable/536729.

[19] Ibid., 333.

[20] Ibid., 334.

[21] Ibid., 334.

[22] "HuffPost - Breaking News, U.S. and World News." *The Huffington Post,* TheHuffingtonPost.com, www.huffingtonpost.com/rev-dr-randy-s-woodley/trail-of-tears-and-christianity-truth_b_1920921.html).

[23] ZEDENO, MARIA-NIEVES, and ROBERT CHRISTOPHER BASALDU. "OZARK NATIONAL SCENIC RIVERWAYS, MISSOURI CULTURAL AFFILIATION STUDY FINAL REPORT." *DELAWARE TRIBE HISTORIC PRESERVATION OFFICE, 95.* dthpo.delawaretribe.org/wp-content/uploads/2012/01/OzarksCAS.pdf.

other Cherokees who had inhabited the area since prehistoric times,[24] thus becoming one of the groups that would later be known as the Western Cherokee.[25] The influence of Christianity and the time gaps that exist between these groups could account for the attitudes that these other Cherokees have towards the rituals as these practices would not be very Christian things to do. On top of this these customs with sex and nudity would most likely be seen as witchcraft by the Holy Rollers in the hills.[26] However, the century of separation, from the 1800s to the early 1900s, between the Cherokee groups in other parts of the Missouri and Arkansas Ozarks and the Cherokees that would become the Cherokee Nation of Oklahoma, later to become known as the Cherokee Nation as they are today, would quite certainly account for the different practices, as this is how cultures work. They still grow and evolve in lieu of each other dependent to the influences around them.

The response by one Cherokee faction when asked about practices done by other Cherokees displays how different groups had their own cultural customs that developed while in seclusion, or a better way to put it is that these cultures changed once separated from the greater tribe, and thus practices became vastly varied between the Cherokee factions by the turn of the 20th century. For instance, Vance Randolph recorded that one group of hill-folk widely practiced driving nails into peach trees, much like how Cherokee's drive coffin nails through goat's hearts to kill witches,[27] and upon his inquiries he was told it was a charm; he could never find the actual reason for the practice though, as he said that the people in the group, "are evasive or noncommittal"

---

[24] Ibid., 95.

[25] Ibid., 95.

[26] Randolph, Vance. "Nakedness in Ozark Folk Belief." *The Journal of American Folklore*, vol. 66, no. 262, 1953, 338. JSTOR, www.jstor.org/stable/536729.

[27] Randolph, Vance. *Ozark Superstitions.* (Dover, 1964), 299.

when he asks them about it.[28] Randolph found this avoidance to the explanation of certain cultural practices to be true even with families he was close with. An old man of another clan, one that Randolph's wife had close ties to, snapped at him for asking as to why the peach tree practice was done stating," Them's family matters,"[29] upset with Randolph, this old man said nothing more about it.

After this interaction, Randolph tried to gather more information on the peach tree custom through means of his wife, but all she could find out further on the matter was that at night one of the daughters of a family would strip down from their nightgown before driving a nail into the tree.[30] Although he did say, that one explanation given for this practice by some other hill folks was that it helped the trees to be more fruitful and retained the fruit until it was ripe.[31] However, this still shows how group customs were done in secret[32] with family traditions closely guarded from their greater communities, being those who were not related to them through kinship or tribal ties, that lived around them even when confronted with the fact that others had knowledge of their practices as well.[33]

Even in the foodways and food taboos Ozark Indians are still easily identifiable by Randolph who makes a distinction between the Indigenous population of the area and the other Anglo communities' personal diets. Vance Randolph states that, "Miss Margaret Lillie, of Rockaway Beach, Missouri, who boasts some Cherokee blood, told me that she had eaten land turtles and that they were very good. Later, I tried one myself, as cooked by

---

[28] Randolph, Vance. "Nakedness in Ozark Folk Belief." *The Journal of American Folklore*, vol. 66, no. 262, 1953, 336. JSTOR, www.jstor.org/stable/536729.
[29] Ibid., 336.
[30] Ibid., 336.
[31] Ibid., 336.
[32] Ibid., 337.
[33] Ibid., 337.

some Indians from Sallisaw, Oklahoma, and found it palatable enough. But I have never known a non-Native American hillbilly who could be induced to taste a land turtle, and the majority of them will not eat any sort of reptile".[34] This statement shows how Indian families maintained their own traditional foodways showing how they were not fully assimilating their diet to that of the average Anglo Ozarker. Even today, many Native American Ozarkers still maintain diets that consist of traditional foods such as bean bread, fried hominy, Sucker fish, grape dumplings, Cherokee bread pudding, Cherokee corn phones, fry bread, kanuchi, wild onions and eggs, and what they call an old field apricot drink, to name a few of the foods consumed.[35]

The fear of removals from the states became a part of the culture because of historical traumas that can also be seen again in the folklife. Randolph talks of an Indigenous family that used nails from a coffin, a goat's heart, and a wire cage to kill a witch that they had believed murdered a family member. In this passage, there is a well-defined fear that is palatable amongst the people involved with the matter, as they take extensive lengths to make sure their family is not mentioned in the retelling of the practice. Vance Randolph writes, "I was told about this by two young, educated members of the family, who gave me permission to publish the story on the condition that no names or identifying data were included." Randolph goes on farther to inquire more about the practice by contacting the man who sold the family the coffin stating, "The man who sold the coffin refused to discuss this particular case but admitted that 'more than once' people had come to his place of business and wanted to pull nails out of coffins in which bodies were lying at the time. The nails, or screws, he thought, were to be used in 'some Indian ceremony.'" Randolph does state that the family that he first discussed the

---

[34] Randolph, Vance. *Ozark Superstitions*. (Dover, 1964), 253.
[35] Cantrell, Doyne, and Ben Stephens. *The Western Cherokee Nation of Arkansas and Missouri: a history: a heritage* (Place of publication not identified: Lulu Publishing, 2009), 67-74.

ritual with did boast of their Cherokee blood however he goes on to say, "the persons concerned in this goats-heart affair have had little contact with Indians; they know nothing of tribal religions or ceremonials, and many of them never even spoke with a fullblood in their lives."[36] This shows how the family in question almost denies any connection to the tribal practices, and yet they have claimed their Native blood to Vance Randolph, an outsider to their community, while at the same time continuing on the rituals within their own homes as they believe them to hold real power. This family with their actions displays how a group can quite literally "hide" in plain sight through denial and omittance in what I would consider a real time example.

The statement made to Vance Randolph by this family about having little contact with Indians could have just as easily been, and most likely was, a lie, since Native Americans were ever present within their area, to keep Randolph away from their tribal affairs just as much as it could be taken as the truth. Without any family names mentioned it is hard to determine just how connected to the tribal ways of life the family in question was; however, the omission of family information could just as easily support the fact that they did have tribal relations they did not want revealed to the outside public. If the statement is true on face value, then the family could have just known about a few ceremonial practices of Native Americans, as a residual trait from having Indian relatives in the past, and still not been tribally affiliated as stated by Randolph. If this is truly the case then it is a strong one for the fact of just how influential Native American practices were in the area, and how they stayed ever present within the descendants of the original Natives. On the other side of the coin, the family could have been, and most likely were, tribally connected Native Americans that were actively trying to protect their group by separating the story from the families through the denial of having knowledge in any Native

---

[36] Randolph, Vance. *Ozark Superstitions.* (Dover, 1964), 299.

religions and ceremonial practices, regardless to the fact that they were currently participating in one in which they were now being asked about from this outsider to their community. This would be and was given the other factors in the situation such as the required anonymity, an example of the etic idea of cultural preservation through denial or omittance of their existence to the Majority. A practice I have discussed earlier through using emic terms such as Black Dutch or the changing of names.

More modern research, done in the 1960s, that came out about the Folklore of the Ozarks tried to separate the people into groups along outdated and binary racial lines, failing to see that there was an overlap between Native Nations and the new settlers in the early days of settlement. More specifically, the development of subcultures within the greater body of peoples that inhabit the geological and cultural areas defined as the Ozarks. These unrepresented Subcultures combine aspects of multiple cultural facets, both Anglo and Native American, and has never been fully represented within the area as a tribal body, the peoples were not given the cultural plurality that was given to the western Indigenous nations such as the Navajo working as ranchers in the 70s, or the "Urban Indians", working in the cities after being forced to relocate off of the Reservations under guidance of federal programs. In this research things such as race and ethnicity were seen to past academics as trivial in means of examination and explanation in terms of identifying the Ozarker's connection to their origins back East. For an example of the shady guess work done we can look at the supported idea for the origins of the Ozarker.

According to the researchers of early Ozarks Studies their source material, is mostly, compiled from Vance Randolph's collected materials on the Ozarks. After reviewing Randolph's writings, the scholars reported that most of the people interviewed had surnames that seemed to be primarily from Anglo-Saxon descent, compiled with court documents and census records which showed the same results of names being, Anglo-Saxon, and thus they theorized then that meant that most Ozarkers are of Anglo origin due to the prevalence of the names. However, this is a fraudulent statement, considering that the widespread use of Anglo names as nicknames was common practice by Natives by the 1840s, add to this the fact that before the removal period a great number of tribal peoples in the southern states had already begun to assimilate to Anglo ways in the 1700s, to include the practice of intermarriage between white and Indian peoples in Appalachia, which would have also provided for Anglo surnames as well, and lastly let us not forget the need for these multicultural Indian groups to conceal their Native American heritage in the Ozarks by adopting more Anglo names to avoid the removals, with these facts it is not hard to see why Natives would have only openly shared a few aspects of their practices alongside their Anglo ways rather than identify as only Native Americans; thus on paper when reviewing the documents discussed, especially from the Alien period on, it would seem as if the population is mostly white. However, that summation is equivalent to saying that because the ground is soaked outside it rained when there are multiple ways that it could have gotten wet, ranging from morning dew to a burst pipe in the road. It is now palpable to see the effects that the binary racial understandings of the times had on the research as it also talks of open intermarriages between Native Americans and whites in the Ozarks, yet they determined these same peoples to then be Anglo do to their surnames, which to me is just ridiculous and quite frankly a contradiction. Anglo surnames were present within native communities as they were first adopted to ease communications in trade after contact, and over the decades of trade the communities formed blood links to whites before they started to migrate into the Ozarks, as well as the fact that once they were in the Ozarks the fullblood families over time had cross cultural ties requiring family names that they had established with some of the Anglo settlers starting back in the 1830s and 1840s leading to the mixed communities that we have today.

Even more proof of this connection can then be found within the words of the folkloric recordings of the Ozarks itself.

Stories of the corn made from flat footed bees refer to the blue corn grown by the Chickasaw. The folklore claims that in the past "some old timers knew no other" in reference to the type of corn they ate; this statement could easily be interpreted to mean that the Old Timers who only knew of the "blue corn" came from, or at least have a strong connection to, the Chickasaw people. So let's check the ballistics here, on one hand you have scholars, who by the 1960s still relied on Vance Randolph's work for the bulk of their research, trying to define the hill people as separate from the "melting pot" of American assimilation claiming that the hills preserved elements of the Anglo groups past heritages and cultures from Europe due to isolation,[37] regardless to Randolph's acknowledgement of a potent Native American presence within the DNA of the area,[38] with an ethnocentric view towards the development of the Ozarks that favored the white cultures over all others; while on the other hand, during this same time period in the 1960s and early 70s, you have the Native tribes within the Ozark Mountains publicly asserting their identities, pushing for the preservation of their existence within the area in their fight for equality, while still being ignored by scholars and the mass American population alike denying these tribes fair representation even further.

In the 1970s, presented with the Civil Rights movement, The American Indian Movement, and the armed standoff at Wounded Knee, the federal government created multiple task forces to address issues that were plaguing Indian country at the time. With the creation of these task forces the goal was to look at issues from an Indian standpoint which led the federal government to enlist the help of Native Americans from around the country. This delegation of Indians included Kathy McKee, who was listed as a Missouri-Cherokee, and Sarah Sneed, who

---

[37] "Immigrants in the Ozarks: a Study in Ethnic Geography." *The Annals of Iowa* 44 (1978), 326-327. https://doi.org/10.17077/0003-4827.11374

[38] Randolph, Vance, and G. Legman. *Unprintable Ozark Folksongs and Folklore.* (University of Arkansas Press, 1992), 12.

was listed as a Cherokee without the Missouri designation; the interesting thing to note here is that not only did Cherokees identify the distinction in the 1800s between the families of the Missouri and Arkansas Cherokees, or the Old Settlers who did not remove, from those who would become registered with the CNO in the 1900s, but also that there is still a distinction made by the federal government between the Natives that are present and organized as tribal peoples within the Missouri Ozarks in the 1960s and 1970s. These people, being Arkansas and Missouri Native Americans involved in the American Indian Movement in the late 60s and 70s, were standing up for their rights in places outside of Oklahoma. This was well before there was a "monetary gain" from being tribally affiliated. Mind you this was happening in places where it took U.S. Army troops to protect the minority students from the majority whites, and in some cases to protect the students from the States own National Guard troops who were called up to keep them off the grounds after the federal courts said that schools had to desegregate,[39] these individuals were not into it for money. They were in a fight for their rights, and sadly to say, their descendants are still in that same fight today.

We can see that regardless to the extreme racism and segregation of the times the Native peoples still in the Missouri and Arkansas Ozarks identified as indigenous, such as the Missouri-Cherokee Kathy McKee, during a period when racial violence was once again at a high point in American society.[40] McKee serving as a Task Force Specialist is also noteworthy as she is among a list of predominate tribal figures of the time who were entrusted to, "conduct a comprehensive review of historical/legal developments underlying the Indian/federal government relationship and to recommend necessary policy revisions. After considering

---

[39] Chadwick, Alex. "Little Rock Remembers Troops' Arrival." *NPR*, NPR, 24 Sept. 2007, www.npr.org/templates/story/story.php?storyId=14654126.
[40] United States, Congress, "Final Report Submitted: to Congress May 17, 1977. Volume One of Two.", 1977, 1–591.

the work of 11 task forces."[41] This was all going on in the late 60s and 70s while Ozark Studies was in its infancy and getting its first look of scholarship into the Immigrants and history of the Ozarks. In 1970 Elmo Ingenthron had his book, *Indians of The Ozark Plateau*, published by School of the Ozarks Press. While this was the first substantial work done on the Indigenous people of the area Elmo still committed the Amish error, as previously discussed, by ignoring the Indigenous groups in the area such as the one Kathy McKee hailed from. Even though there was ample evidence of the presence of Native Americans still organized as tribal communities within the Ozarks when Elmo conducted his field work, he still never reached out to any of them. Instead, he decided to dedicate the last chapter of his book to the "Indian Contributions to Ozarkian Culture" failing to understand that the Indigenous and their cultures were still ever present. Elmo however was far from the only one to make this mistake.

In 1976, Rüssel Gerlach, then a professor at Southwest Missouri State University drafted his book, *Immigrants in the Ozarks,* which then became known by scholars as a work that lays out a concise historical cultural geographical examination of the area. This book was given praise by scholars in its day for its coverage of the past immigrations into southern Missouri however it only gave focus to the arrival of the first Europeans. The book defined these Anglo groups as distinct ethnic enclaves in modern times claiming that in the Ozark mountains heritage and culture managed to avoid the "melting pot" experience of assimilation that is often found in immigrant groups of the past from Europe as they integrated into mass American society. With no regard for the Native American groups present in the area, the only immigrants that Gerlach studied were Anglo descendants being those of German, Poles, Swiss, Italians, Mennonites, and Amish heritages. He went over the experiences of the German immigrants and development of their group, including the expansion

---

[41] Ibid., 6.

of their settlements, their agricultural practices, and their religion, language, and general attitudes.

In Gerlach's work he covers the patterns of settlement within the region by select European groups, the Amish, and the Mennonites. Gerlach's findings were that while a degree of assimilation had occurred in the Ozark Highland, no major immigrant group could in the Ozarks could be, conveniently considered, as part of the "melting pot" stereotype, and this was written by him in the 1970s. So, this raises the question as to how is it that the Anglo groups stayed as distinguished populations, but the Native American groups did not even though the groups were under similar circumstances? It seems to me that these Europeans were given the right to cultural pluralism as their societies remained distinct in their religion, agriculture, architecture, and the value they placed on land and homes while the Non Anglo groups were not based solely on racially driven motives.[42] This was regardless to the fact that Native American groups were present, and even serving in federal task forces during the time of Gerlach's fieldwork, yet for whatever reason they were not included in the history of the Ozarks and have been kept out of the annals since; to include the modern works written by leading Ozark scholars today such as the book, *A History of the Ozarks, Volume 1: The Old Ozarks,* by Brooks Blevins in where he praises the White Settlers, and once again equates the indigenous peoples to a thing of the past, with the author focusing mostly on the white populations to better their image and move away from the ignorant poor white Ozark stereotypes that have been ever so present in popular culture. They were, and still are, denied the cultural pluralism that was, and still is, given to the European settlers in the Ozarks; ultimately erasing them from the view of current American political matters within the state and thus becoming the targets of federally recognized Indians who

---

[42] "Immigrants in the Ozarks: a Study in Ethnic Geography." *The Annals of Iowa* 44 (1978), 326-327. https://doi.org/10.17077/0003-4827.11374

serve within the state governments; such as Rocky Miller who is a Missouri Statesman, a Member of the Cherokee Nation, and a person who is adamantly against any recognition of the groups within the state,[43] leaving these Native factions to fall through the cracks.

Another thing to note is that the Ozarks have been a bastion of extremism and violence since their inception into American society, continuing throughout the Civil War, and on. The history of the Ozarks shows how race has been an elemental issue showing how by being a part of these federal task forces Missouri Natives were taking a position against their oppressors in the state governments. While tribes, such as the southern Cherokee that once rode under the rebel flag in the war between the states, now faced racial bigotry and persecution under those same stars and bars. At the turn of the century organizations such as the KKK had almost free roam in the South as they chased out, and killed, the non-whites in their areas of influence. Historically, people in the Ozarks have been conditioned to ignore bigotry displayed to the people of color around them, and as a result tended to do so well into Jim Crow and after. So much so in fact that in the early 1900s, more than 1,000 Black residents fled from the outlining area of Harrison, Arkansas, due to racism after the Elaine Massacre created a situation that was so intense that it was dangerous for anyone of color to be out after nightfall.[44]

In Arkansas there are extremist Christian groups, which believe in a land ruled by God's law calling for the execution of people based on offenses such as blasphemy, abortion, or the sin of same-sex activity, which have developed within the states bounds and still thrive until today. Sadly, one can see this overt hate in real time when they drive past billboards in Arkansas

----

[43] "Missouri Lawmakers Try to Define Real Native American Art." *Cherokee Phoenix,* www.cherokeephoenix.org/Article/index/11983.
[44] Stockley , Grif. "Elaine Massacre of 1919." Encyclopedia of Arkansas, www.encyclopediaofarkansas.net/encyclopedia/entry-detail.aspx?entryID=1102.

that state, "Anti-Racist is code for Anti-White."[45] The town of Harrison is still primarily white with only 34 African-American people out of its 13,000 population that resides there, it is host to the headquarters of The Knights of the Ku Klux Klan,[46] and in 2013 Harrison was given the unofficial title of America's most hateful small town according to the Southern Poverty Law Center.[47] With this amount of unchallenged racism in the past, and present, that was, and in part still is, supported by the white politicians who created the social policies within the Ozarks based upon racist views, and the lingering existence of the overtly racist traditions within the states today, one can see how it would have been far safer to hide in seclusion in groups as Native Americans within the bounds of the states rather than face the accepted and lawful hate that strangles the region.

Along with the long-standing tradition of race-based hate towards minority groups within the Ozarks, it should also be stated that there is a long-standing, and well-funded, tradition of political corruption that has been a constant within both the Arkansas and Missouri State governments. So bad was this political corruption that in the past private armies have been raised by political factions and used in Lieu of the law. In Arkansas there has been times where individual citizens were rostered into battalions in support of politicians, who then incited coups, that resulted in the violent storming of the Arkansas Statehouse.[48] To

---

[45] Morris, Frank. "Tale Of Two Billboards: An Ozark Town's Struggle To Unseat Hate." NPR, NPR, 12 May 2014, www.npr.org/2014/05/12/311107696/tale-of-two-billboards-an-ozark-towns-struggle-to-unseat-hate).

[46] Nolan, Hamilton. "Ku-Klux-Klan." Gawker, 3 Apr. 2012, gawker.com/tag/ku-klux-klan.

[47] Bella, Timothy. "In Arkansas, White Town Is a Black Mark." *Al Jazeera America*, 10 Dec. 2014, america.aljazeera.com/articles/2014/12/10/harrison-arkansashategroups.html.

48 RECONSTRUCTION AND THE BROOKS-BAXTER WAR 1865-1874." *Old State House Museum,* www.oldstatehouse.com/About-Us/History-of-the-Old-State-House/reconstruction-and-the-brooks-baxter-war-1865-1874.

put this in perspective, starting as early as the 1830s the Native peoples within the bounds of both Arkansas and Missouri had been overran by westward expansion and told to leave the lands or face punishment by their political and social oppressors because of their race, thus the Natives had to choose between leaving their lands or to hideout and risk punishment; the result was that some groups of Indians left while others chose the latter and stayed. Those that left continued relationships with the Federal government in what is now present-day Oklahoma. Those that chose to stay then lost that connection to the federal government. Now moving on past the Civil War most of the Native populations at this point had spent more than forty years in hiding. The Native populations had also been further strained by the Civil War with groups siding along with both the Northern and the Southern factions. With the development of vigilante justice, such as the Baldknobbers, who terrorized the lands at night lynching people in the areas surrounding the White River, while other vigilante groups operated in the same fashion across the Ozarks, made their personal safety an added reason for natives to continue the need to stay secluded as the land became almost lawless for everyone living there. It was known that while some "Ozarkians with Indian wives managed to find, "both social and economic advantages in the new territory" once they moved to Oklahoma; those that didn't remove found themselves to be outlaws or, "fugitives from Ozark justice."[49]

On the broader political spectrum, the native populations had seen corruption that was rampant in the reconstruction-era in Arkansas. Even the folks that could pass as white often times still could not vote in the state as a lot of Native Ozarkers were ex confederates soldiers; in the cases where they had fought for the North, they often had family members who fought for,

---

[49] Ingenthron, Elmo. *Indians of the Ozark Plateau*. (The School of The Ozarks Press, 1970), 159.

or supported, the South in the war of the states and thus were considered Southern sympathizers regardless to their own service to the Union, disenfranchised from the government, and barred from voting. The Political problems and corruption blew up into the Brooks-Baxter War. In 1872, the populations watched as the federal government did relatively nothing to prevent corruption in the State House as this election produced the illegitimate Governorship of Elisha Baxter, this was because there was widespread election fraud that occurred during the election process; a practice which seemed to be embedded within Arkansas's state's political history until about 1970, and depending on how you feel about the Clinton & Rose law firm scandals,[50] some could argue it went on much longer, with the rural areas such as the Ozarks, where most of the poor whites and natives lived, being manipulated the most at the polls at the Arkansas Statehouse. Brooks had appealed the results of the election and he was found to be the rightful person to hold the Governor's office after the Pulaski County Circuit Court of Judge John Whytock declared him the true governor of the State. Brooks however, regardless to being the rightful governor, lost favor during the battle and was still ousted by Federal troops who then reinstated Baxter in the end.[51]

Corruption in politics continued across the southern states. With the development of Jim Crow Laws that benefited whites, and the lack of work within the Ozarks, more hardships came around about the turn of the century for tribal peoples as, "The region experienced significant rural population losses between 1900 and 1940. Some people moved to cities such as Fayetteville,

---

[50] "Whitewater Special Report: Whitewater Timeline." *The Washington Post,* WP Company, www.washingtonpost.com/wp-srv/politics/special/whitewater/timeline.htm.

[51] RECONSTRUCTION AND THE BROOKS-BAXTER WAR 1865-1874." *Old State House Museum,* www.oldstatehouse.com/About-Us/History-of-the-Old-State-House/reconstruction-and-the-brooks-baxter-war-1865-1874.

Harrison, or Little Rock, while others left Arkansas entirely. These population losses were exacerbated in the Depression, as those that were unable to pay taxes were forced to leave their land and homes.[52] As a result a lot of Tribal governments made changes to their lifestyles to adapt to the times. They had to evolve to that of both a static society, by maintaining the small farms that they could use in their original areas, while also venturing out as nomadic elements when the younger abled bodied people would go off to follow the crops as migrant workers throughout the seasons creating Kinship Networks all the way out to the west coast. For example, my family's experience during this time was spent moving from the Midwest to the west coast and back in a cyclical fashion. After losing the family farm in Arkansas, in the 1920s to racism, my great grandfather Talmadge Moore was forced with his siblings away from subsistence farming and hunting into the lives of migrant workers. They would move as a family as well as with other cousins, three families altogether in one caravan to be exact, often sharing one small house at the farm once they arrived. To put this into perspective, they would move across the nation looking for work on a yearly basis after spending winter hunting in the Ozarks of Arkansas, moving to tend corn fields on farms in the Oklahoma Ozarks, continuing in the fall to pick apples in the San Joaquin Valley of California, and then coming back to Arkansas or Oklahoma for the winter once more. The tribes claim that during this time they would hold annual meetings, such as homecomings or ceremonies, to handle tribal business.[53] Often these events would be held around the time of a harvest in various locations throughout the Ozarks. The Salyerville Indians also displayed the same type of migration patterns in their movements from Appalachia across the Ohio River

---

[52] Baker, William. *Public Schools in the Ozarks, 1920-40*. Arkansas Historic Preservation Program, www.arkansaspreservation.com/_literature_133242/Public_Schools_in_the_Ozarks,1920-40.

[53] Pavlik, Steve, and Robert K. Thomas. *A Good Cherokee, a Good Anthropologist: Papers in Honor of Robert K. Thomas*. (American Indian Studies Center, 1998), 70.

Valley, for a look at this we can reference Richard Carlson in where he states,

> In the case of the Salyersville Indians, social and economic cooperation, and long-term obligation to 'kin' typically outweighs short-term obligation or economic advantages for self. For example, during the Thacker Coal Town years in the 1900s teens and twenties, or the following era of working on the Midwest muck fields, most Salyersville Indians undertook such work 'abroad' in large clusters of interrelated family groups. Such mechanisms have provided the means to maintain their large families and deal with changing social relations even in the direst scenarios. And while many people have 'dropped off over the years and have moved away and lost touch with the core of their Indigenous family relations, enough have adhered to commitment toward kin to retain the Salyersville Indians' distinctiveness as a group. Indeed, some outsiders still characterize us as a 'clannish' people who 'stick to their own'

Just as the Salyersville Indians split off in clusters so did these Ozark Native American groups. Yearly they would come back and meet. These homecomings created new kinship networks as Homecomings continue currently as a tradition in most of the tribes today. At the turn of the century tribes stayed to themselves; They continued hiding in the hills even after being recognized as United States citizens in 1924, because fifth-teen years earlier, in 1909, it was once again reaffirmed through legislation that legally within the state of Missouri it was still unlawful to be Indian, in fact the informants were even rewarded by being given 50% of the goods that were left by the Indian family reported, while on the other hand, these Indians were forcibly removed or killed for their infractions.[54] Once again the infraction

------

[54] Good, Judy. "MISSOURI INDIAN LAWS." *Roots Web*, sites.rootsweb.com/~moccga/moIndianLaw.html.

that was being committed was that of being Native American and living within the state of Missouri. To speak to the perspective of the native peoples that stayed in hiding, with only a few of the more brazen families overtly practicing their ways in the Alien Era, and later during the times of Jim Crow, secrecy seemed like the only option for them to maintain their autonomy as they had no representation by this point in either of the state governments, add in the fact that these communities internalized a fear towards outsiders from close to one hundred years of oppression on their backs within the Ozarks, with no end to the hate in sight, and it is easy to see why this decision was made.

In both Missouri and Arkansas, the Ozark societies have had a long-standing position among the citizens, both politically and socially, that seems to translate into a willingness to ignore a person's faults and their transgressions, no matter what they are, if they do not affect them directly as an individual. I can make this statement because both states have been filled in the past with crony politics, extreme racism, and classism, in where the needs of others, more specifically the needs of the poor and minority communities, went ignored, and thus by the mid-20th century, with the rise of the Pendergast Political Machine in Missouri, the majority Native communities had their just fears towards the ethnocentric Whites who ruled both the federal and state governments.

It is disheartening for anyone to see people take that of a passive position towards a person whose wrongdoings were at the expense of others, especially when the person is a known criminal, like Tom Pendergast. One could also argue that when it came to minorities and their basic human rights people took this passive approach across the southern states as seen with Jim Crow which allowed for a whole host of atrocities to be committed against communities with established minority populations. Such is the case of what would become known as the Rosewood massacre, which took place in 1923 when a relatively well-off town in Florida, that was predominantly black, had a chain of events start to happen on New Year's Day that would end with this town being wiped, "off the map, with the families who lived there so terrified to speak of what happened that the town was almost wiped from history, too."[55] The whole event started because a female named Frannie Taylor, who was a resident of the close by town of Sumner, where many of the African-Americans from Rosewood worked, "brought neighbors running to her door on the morning of January 1. Taylor had been beaten, her face visibly bruised, and she claimed her attacker was Black. Eyewitness accounts from her domestic workers told a different story; they said she was struck during an argument with the white lover she was seeing while her husband was at work."[56] As violence against colored folk was commonplace in the 1920s, only a few white people helped when this mob stormed into the town, "despite national publicity about what was, at the time, called the 'Rosewood riots.' Those who failed to act included the governor of Florida; in fact, he offered to help the county sheriff," who was allowing a mob to ruthlessly attack innocent people, "who declined assistance. Reassured that the matter had been well handled, the governor headed out for a lazy round of golf."[57] totally disregarding the black men, woman, and children who were terrorized, with some of the people being murdered for the infidelities of a married white woman, by this unruly mob that the law was in full support of.

During the 1920s, it was common for poor whites to be neglected by the federal government as well due to their economic struggles during the depression. A prime example of this is the Bonus Army, which was made up of an estimated 43,000 with 17,000 being U.S. World War I veterans, and the rest of the army consisting of their families, and a host of affiliated groups.

---

[55] Gilligan, Heather. "A White Mob Wiped This All-Black Florida Town off the Map. 60 Years Later Their Story Was Finally..." *Timeline*, 4 Apr. 2018, timeline.com/all-black-town-rosewood-wiped-off-the-map-by-white-mob-73ca6630802b.

[56] Ibid.

[57] Ibid.

The goal of this Bonus army was to be given their cash-payment redemption as promised to them for fighting over seas by the federal government. They gathered in Washington, D.C., this took place during the summer of 1932, and ultimately resulted in a great number of wounded veterans with a few dead after police and federal troops descended on the Bonus Army's encampment.[58] So then it is understandable that during this time the Native American communities kept their distance from others, especially the state and federal governments, seeing as they did not have their own armies, or even a police force to protect them on the most basic level, and if 43,000 Americans, to include over 17,000 veterans, couldn't get what was owed to their families then what chance did Ozark Indians have at getting a fair shake in Congress?

Just as in Florida, white men ran the governments of Arkansas and Missouri, and by the 1930s Missouri's crony politics had extended into arms of the federal government as well, as Pendergast had connections to Harry Truman. This was a strong relationship that Pendergast held with Truman, to the point that when even after he learned about his transgressions Truman still stated, "He was always my friend and I have always been his." This statement was made after Truman, in the midst of WWII while serving as a vice President of America, made time out of his schedule to attend Tom Prendergast's funeral in 1945.[59] This insured the Native Americans in the Ozarks that the federal government would continue on to accept political corruption as by the end of WWII Truman was president and the Natives in both states lost trust in all forms of US Government, both State and Federal, once more. Moving into the 1950's, with the lack of population because of migration behaviors of the peoples due to economic stress, and the lack of representation in the state

---

[58] DEste, Carlo. *Eisenhower: a Soldiers Life.* (Owl Books, 2003), 223.
[59] "Jackson Democratic Club." *Truman Places*, www.trumanlibrary.org/places/kc8.htm.

governments, the Natives that stayed within the states became generally, in terms of outside appearances, assimilated with the mountain life of the broader community, as a continued attempt from them to stay in the area. The communities' Native practices and traditions continued to stay in seclusion until around the start of the Civil Rights Movement when Native groups once again became more active in the Ozarks and by the 1980s tribes, bands, and the family groups that had been in hiding in the past started to proclaim their existence revolting against their oppressors on the state government level.

In Missouri, the Cherokees made strives within the state to reconstruct the relationship between the state government and the Indigenous nations before applying for federal recognition. However, this was before inter-tribal disputes caused the greater tribal body to fracture. During the 1980s Native American people, like Ray Lovan, started to openly admit to their heritage in public. Lovan talks of her Choctaw heritage stating, "early settlers," in the White River area, "were Alabeth (Ball) Freeman who with her husband Aaron Freeman, were my great, great grandparents. She was a half-blood Choctaw, and they owned an improvement in Mississippi Choctaw Nation." She also goes over the family's migration into the area stating, "They left Mississippi and went to North Carolina in 1831. In or about 1839 they and some relatives came to the Ozarks and located at a large spring at Topaz on North Fork and put up a grist mill and a distillery."[60] Lovan here, speaks to her heritage when just a generation earlier to do so would have been met with racial backlash. While race and class relations are still ever present in our modern-day politics, at least now the peoples are speaking to their own existences, and that is saying a lot in comparison to one hundred years ago.

---

[60] Lovan, Ray. "The Early Settlement of The North Fork Area in the Eastern Part of Douglas County, Missouri." *White River Valley Historical Quarterly*, vol. 9, no. 1, 1985, thelibrary.org/lochist/periodicals/wrv/V9/N1/f85e.htm.

FOR THE LOVE OF
MONEY AND POWER

In our current times the Cherokee Nation, as a tribal body, spends millions in lawyer fees to go after what they call "fraudulent groups." While there are self-proclaimed entities, like the groups that can be found in the streets of New Orleans[61], that in no way means that all are, as many Cherokee factions over the chorus of space and time became inter displaced peoples who are currently still trying to get federally recognized. Yet, over the past decade the Cherokee Nation has taken to making it a "us" against "them" endeavor between the recognized and unrecognized factions of Cherokee peoples to ensure their position as gatekeepers and maintain their power as federally recognized Cherokee groups by the federal government, and thus, the only Cherokees entitled to the rights that come with that designation. To do so the Cherokee Nation has enlisted the help of the other federally recognized Cherokee groups as well. In our current times Federally recognized Cherokee factions all admit that there are many people of Cherokee Ancestry and Blood that are not enrolled for many various reasons; yet they actively fight these people in regards to recognition as can be seen when the Cherokee Nation and the Eastern Band of Cherokee Indians signed in resolutions to oppose and denounce state and federal recognition of any new Cherokee tribes or bands.[62] The tribes also donate each year to both state and federal politicians to obtain their political ends. The Cherokee Nation to protect its political

---

[61] Sakakeeny, Matt. "Mardi Gras Indians - Know Louisiana." *64 Parishes*, 21 Feb. 2020, https://64parishes.org/entry/mardi-gras-indians.

[62] "A Resolution Opposing Fabricated Cherokee 'Tribes.'" *Indianz.com*, www.indianz.com/boardx/topic.asp?TOPIC_ID=33699.

interests has even invested money to go after their own citizens in the past when monetary issues are involved such as gaming, as seen in the recent case with Oklahoma Gov. Kevin Stitt, in which their attorneys said that his family only has one tie to the Cherokee Dawes Rolls;[63] and there is probable cause that it was fraudulent, however, his family's accused fraudulent enrollment only came out in an attempt to drag his name through the mud over gaming disputes. The failed attempt to disenroll his family from the tribe happened one hundred years ago. These tactics are done as the Cherokee Nation was, and is, a "to big to fail" oligarchy run by elites who are motivated by money and power, as I will prove later that the Cherokee Nation constantly picks and chooses documents and events to lay claim to heritage and property, yet most of their base documents are faulty at best.

In recent years, the Eastern Band of Cherokee Indians have been taken under the wing of the Cherokee Nation since the signing of the resolutions, and recently was called out for their actions with U.S. Senator Richard Burr commenting on their less than straight forward dealings on matters that have to do with gaming as well stating, "Indian gaming generates more than $105 billion in economic output each year. In North Carolina, where gaming is strictly regulated at the state level, the state's only two casinos are operated by the Cherokee. A growing economy and a lack of competition have been good for business. Last year, the Cherokee announced record-breaking profits and advanced a $250 million expansion of their Cherokee County casino. The tribe also donates hundreds of thousands of dollars each year to North Carolina politicians with little scrutiny. Whereas political action committees and office holders like myself file electronic financial disclosure reports that are easily searchable

---

[63] Graham Lee Brewer Feb. 24, 2020 Like Tweet Email Print Subscribe Donate Now. "The Cherokee Nation Once Fought to Disenroll Gov. Kevin Stitt's Ancestors." *High Country News – Know the West*, 24 Feb. 2020, https://www.hcn. org/articles/indigenous-affairs-the-cherokee-nation-once-fought-to-disenroll-gov-kevin-stitts-ancestors.

online and fully transparent, the Cherokee file paper reports that are harder to track. According to one review by a campaign finance watchdog, the Cherokee gave $1.3 million in campaign contributions over the last three elections. That makes them one of the biggest and most powerful political donors in the state. In 2018 alone, the tribe donated nearly $360,000 to lawmakers in the North Carolina General Assembly. Their sway was evident when many of those lawmakers then signed the Cherokee's letter opposing the Catawba gaming facility. I have witnessed the Cherokee's aggressive tactics for years in my work with the Lumbees. The Lumbees are the largest American Indian tribe in the Eastern United States, and they have sought federal recognition since the 1880s. The federal government finally acknowledged them as a tribe in the 1950s but denied them the full benefits and services that other tribes receive. I've worked to help fix this injustice, but the Cherokee have long lobbied against Lumbee recognition because they view it as a threat to their federal benefits and gaming business."[64]

To maintain their power and economic growth the Cherokee Nation, located in Oklahoma, works in unison with the Eastern Band to ensure their supremacy. They do this by claiming that "Fraudulent groups passing themselves off as tribes have become big business during the past two decades, with more than two hundred that claim to be some sort of Cherokee tribe. However, there are only three federally recognized Cherokee tribes: two are in Oklahoma and one in North Carolina. Many of the would-be Cherokee 'tribes' are cultural societies or history clubs, whose members may or may not belong to any of the federally recognized tribes. Still others are harmful, and some

----

[64] Burr, Richard. "Richard Burr: Cherokee Indians Are Bullying Other NC Tribes." *Charlotteobserver*, Charlotte Observer, 19 June 2019, www.charlotteob-server.com/opinion/op-ed/article231717118.html.

are even created for criminal purposes."[65] Statements made like this by federally recognized groups paint the picture that no one other than the three federally recognized tribes are real Cherokees. However, as we have gone over extensively, historically the Cherokees have categorized themselves as different tribes and bands with varying degrees of regulation over the governance of their people in the Cherokee confederacy, with groups in multiple locations who have remnants that in many cases are still in existence today. The blunt lie here, as the Cherokee Nation has it framed, is that there have only been unrecognized tribes as of recently, that these groups have only come about within the past 3 decades, and that all of them are fraudulent.

The Recognized groups try to suggest that these Unrecognized tribal bodies are just a way for whites to capitalize on being Indigenous person by getting people to pay dues into their groups for their own personal gains. However, at its core the past statement is not true. First, we can address why dues are charged to begin with. Most groups have strict requirements that they hold for membership that must be met before an individual can join. For those that do charge a fee it is often associated with the research that it takes to confirm that new members meet the requirements, as it takes a labor of love for their communities, but these resources are not free, thus the need for a fee, as someone must do the work. This is not a new practice as other tribes in the past, which have since been State recognized, have also took the same route as they have required members to pay dues as well. The Indian Club that was the precursor to what is now the Haliwa-Saponi tribe is a perfect example of how the resources collected were utilized in the 1950s as the, "donations collected at early Club meetings went to conduct research on

---

[65] "What Is a Real Indian Nation? What Is a Fake Tribe? (Cherokee TV)." PUMABydesign001's Blog, 31 May 2012, pumabydesign001.com/2012/05/31/ what-is-a-real-indian-nation-what-is-a-fake-tribe-cherokee-tv/.

the group's Indian ancestry and to pay white lawyers to correct their vital documents", and by November of 1953, "the Club authorized the Board of Committees to hire lawyer and state representative, William W. Taylor, Jr., for $100.00, in order to do research on their Indian background."[66] The point stands that money charged by a group for admin tasks does not mean that the group is nefarious in their intent. Lastly, to address the point made of the tribes being new, just coming into existence over the past few decades, this is not the case by any means. Just because groups may reorganize under different names or leadership over the course of their histories does not take away from the fact that they have maintained their core communities continuously since the late 1700s and early 1800s.

In 1978, there was an in-depth study done on some of the Cherokee Communities in the South by Robert K. Thomas. This study listed over a dozen communities that have possessed an amalgamated culture with at least two tribes being represented amongst the peoples, such as the mixed Delaware and Cherokee community in West Virginia. He lists these groups that can be found all over the states located in places such as Alabama, Arkansas, California, Florida, Georgia, Kentucky, Missouri, North Carolina, Ohio, Oklahoma, South Carolina, Tennessee, Texas, Virginia, and West Virginia.[67] The study talked with both recognized and unrecognized tribes that historically, and still, have members that identify as Cherokee among them.[68] This study also thoroughly establishes that unrecognized Cherokee groups are far from new. I can promise you that these Indigenous people did not live their secluded rural lives, often being forced to

---

[66] Richardson, Marvin M. "RACIAL CHOICES: THE EMERGENCE OF THE HALIWA-SAPONI INDIAN TRIBE, 1835-1971." *Carolina Digital Repository*, 151. cdr.lib.unc.edu/indexablecontent/uuid:5211232d-556b-4793-82d3-e5a78baa8a17.

[67] Cherokee Communities Of The South." *The Melungeon Indians*, historical-melungeons.com/rk_thomas.html.

[68] Ibid.

live in poverty, facing racial discrimination and violence, not adopting fully to the Anglo cultures around them, in which they were seen as second-class citizens, just in the hopes that someday it might be lucrative for their great-great grandchildren. Furthermore, the logic of the statement made by the Cherokee Nation, being that because these tribes are recognized they are the only ones that are truly Cherokee people, does not hold water when looking at their own histories. This is because by this same train of thought one could make the argument that the Eastern Band of Cherokee Indians, who use the 1924 Baker Roll to determine membership, and the Keetoowah Band whose Base Roll was made in 1949, would have been considered fraudulent or fake tribes as they were unrecognized factions of Cherokee themselves after the creation of the Cherokee Nation of Oklahoma in 1906.

The argument for denial of unrecognized groups is, as it has been presented by the Cherokee Nation, that by not removing to Indian territory the Cherokees who stayed behind gave up their rights as tribally affiliated Indians. With that said, some of the Old Settlers, as we have covered earlier, did not remove, and thus stayed as smaller Cherokee groups in Missouri and Arkansas. Creating a situation in where they did not become fully enfranchised peoples in the United States, and there for became marginalized and muted in the process, or what the United Nation refers to as Inter Displaced Peoples.[69] The United States Government made no effort to contact or hold open any communications with the rest of the tribe that stayed behind in their old lands as it would have been counterproductive to their cause, just as they had done with other tribal populations elsewhere. However, I would like to state that lack of contact on the part of an Indigenous group should not constitute for denial of heritage and tribal identity from the government as it has not been a

----

[69] "Questions and Answers about Idps." *OHCHR*, https://www.ohchr.org/EN/Issues/IDPersons/Pages/Issues.aspx#4.

disqualifier for other tribes that have been federally recognized in the past.

Now it should be noted that the Cherokee Nation at the turn of the century was dissolved and reformed encompassing many other non-Cherokee Indigenous groups into their ranks within the process. This reformed "Cherokee Nation of Oklahoma" was not governed by its peoples but in fact by the federal government. This was done by Presidentially appointed Chiefs, to do the bidding for the federal government like signing documents, acting as figure heads, sometimes for only a day, from 1906 until 1971. It's known that by 1936, 50% of Cherokees had left Oklahoma looking for work on the west coast in states like Arizona, California, and Oregon.[70] By 1962 only 10% of the Cherokee enrolled with the Nation lived or participated in communal Cherokee life,[71] and in 1968 the Cherokee Nation government only had three employees, it wasn't until 1975 with the enactment of "The Self-Determination Act" that the Cherokee Nation was considered a sovereign tribal body from the United States. the Cherokee chieftains, during the years of being used as federal government Patsies until 1975,[72] may have looked like they worked for their peoples, but they were still governed by the will of the P.O.T.U.S., much like how a Chief of Staff would function, and during this time these men did not lead a standalone sovereign government as the President appointed the Chiefs.[73]

As the biggest tribe in America today the Cherokee have become synonymous with the federal acknowledgment process

---

[70] Smith, Chadwick Corntassel. *Leadership Lessons from the Cherokee Nation: Learn from All I Observe*. (McGraw-Hill Education, 2013), 2.

[71] Wahrhaftig, Albert L. "The Tribal Cherokee Population of Eastern Oklahoma." *Current Anthropology*, vol. 9, no. 5, Part 2, 1968, pp. 510–518., doi:10.1086/200948.

[72] Smith, Chadwick Corntassel. *Leadership Lessons from the Cherokee Nation: Learn from All I Observe*. (McGraw-Hill Education, 2013), 3.

[73] *Appointed Chiefs*, www.cherokee.org/About-The-Nation/History/Chiefs/Appointed-Chiefs.

and thus the gatekeepers of Cherokee history and heritage even though not all Cherokee factions have been federally recognized. They actively try to keep the process hard so that only select groups make the cut, often those that fit into the stereotypes of the Plains and Southwestern Indian cultures. Now it seems to me to be awful hypocritical to require other groups of indigenous peoples to show documents of governance as continuous Nations spanning over hundreds of years, often in places where their histories were not recorded, when the biggest tribe in the United States of America, being the Cherokee Nation, hasn't even done so themselves due to the fact that their own tribe wasn't led by their peoples, but in fact was led by the commander-in-chief of the United States of America through presidential appointees for over a half a century, and thus the Cherokee Nation was not sovereign until it was re-ratified in 1975.[74] So in reality, as far as governance goes, this would make them, contrary to popular belief, one of the youngest sovereign Nations in America. If the Cherokee Nation could lose such political grasp on its peoples, to require presidential appointees to act as chiefs for the span of 70 years after the shutdown of their tribal government at the turn of the 20th century, then why should smaller groups be expected to have retained their public sovereignty on paper when faced with what was then a rise in the oppression against minority groups through segregation? If anything, an Indigenous group should have to show their governance back to the 1970s; because this is when the Cherokee Nation and other federally recognized tribes[75] were re-established. But that is not how it is now because of the influence the federally recognized Cherokee have on the process. The long-standing relationship

---

[74] Smith, Chadwick Corntassel. *Leadership Lessons from the Cherokee Nation: Learn from All I Observe*. (McGraw-Hill Education, 2013), 3.

[75] Adams, Mikaëla."Residency and Enrollment: Dispora and The Catawba Indian Nation." *The South Carolina Historical Magazine*, vol. 113, (South Carolina Historical Society, 2012), 24-49.

between the Cherokee Nation and the United States has created a situation wherein they have a peer-to-peer relationship, gate-keeping those who they see as lesser than tribes for a spot at the table for some help.

So my question then is, how is it that the bad ethnographic research done by non-native scholars at the turn of the century, became considered legitimate and irrefutably valid, regardless to known issues, like that of the Dawes Rolls for example, to be used to establish the grounds of Native American Nations, Like the CN and EBCI, but the scores of good ethnographic fieldwork that has been done since are often scrutinized when presented to the BIA by members of these same federally rec-ognized tribes, who mind you, have their own base rolls that have histories that are rocky in the first place? How is it that the Members of federally recognized tribes, who have personal interests in the matter, get to decide whose history is real just because they hold government positions, and are given prefer-ence to gain said employment as federally recognized members of tribes, or in other words as "real" Indians, within the BIA? For example, the Eastern Band of Cherokee Indians feels that their personal research constitutes more validity on their part than other scholars who are not native.

The Eastern Band of Cherokee Indians believe they have more legitimacy than the anthropologists and the politicians, which represent their constituents of Indian heritage, in North Carolina based solely on the fact that they hold status as a fed-erally recognized tribe. The worst part about this is how the Eastern Band of Cherokee Indians constantly make bad histor-ical claims such as, "Mayas and Aztecs were the descendants of the Cherokees AND that the Cherokees were the first people in the world to grow corn, beans and squash", which is blatantly not true.[76] Another example of federally recognized Cherokee's

---

[76] Thornton, Richard. "Two Different Versions of Cherokee History Collide." *People of One Fire,* 27 Nov. 2017, peopleofonefire.com/cherokee_history_collides.html.

steam rolling smaller tribes can be seen with the Yuchi. Often the word Tennessee is credited to be a Cherokee word, but the Cherokees argue that they have since forgotten what it meant.[77] In reality, Tennessee is a Yuchean word that means "confluence of streams,"[78] and the word had nothing to do with the Cherokee or the Creek as other scholars have claimed in the past. The prejudices that the Eastern Band and the Cherokee Nation hold towards other non-recognized Cherokee groups can be seen on full display in a statement made by the Eastern Band in 2015.

In an article about a bill that was being proposed for the federal recognition of the Lumbee the Eastern Band of Cherokee Indians stated their views towards the State recognized indigenous communities in North Carolina. Based on the fact that they hold the idea that the Lumbees are non-authentic Indian peoples, and with blatant disregard for the scholarly work that has been done in the past to explain the historical development and base culture of the Lumbee, the Eastern Band of Cherokee Indians made this statement, "Following the non-Indian research, the Lumbee have claimed to be 'Croatan' (based on a Lost Colony of Roanoke theory, now disproven), 'Siouan' (a Native language family, not a tribe), Tuscarora, Cheraw, and Cherokee. In fact, for forty years, the Lumbee sought to appropriate Cherokee identity and claimed to be a Cherokee tribe, over our strong objections," the Eastern Band continued on to say, "Based on our review of the history and record, the Eastern Band questions whether the Lumbee can demonstrate that they descend from the Cheraw or any historical tribe".[79] However, scholarly research done in the 20th and 21st centuries has proven that not only do the Lumbee tribe indeed come from a "historical" tribe

---

[77] Elcome, Cary. *What Is the Meaning of the Word "Tennessee"?* 8 Dec. 2019, www.quora.com/What-is-the-meaning-of-the-word-Tennessee.

[78] *Spread the Word -- 4th Annual Yuchi Gathering!,* yuchi.org/spreadtheword.htm.

[79] McKie, Scott. "EBCI Stands Firmly against Lumbee Recognition." *The Cherokee One Feather,* 12 Jan. 2015, theonefeather.com/2015/01/ebci-stands-firmly-against-lumbee-recognition/.

of Indians, but that they are in fact a multicultural indigenous group, claiming their heritage and practices through the Cheraw peoples, the Hatteras Indians, and from a migration of a known Native American cohesive social group of 25-40 families who came to Edgecombe and Granville counties of North Carolina in the 1700s.

History shows that the Indians who migrated into Edgecombe and Granville counties originally were inter displaced peoples from the Virginia Tidewater areas as well as from other smaller tribal groups found in the Coastal and Eastern parts of North Carolina; mostly these Indians came as three small remnant groups of the Yawpim and Potoskite of northeastern North Carolina, and the Nansemond tribe of Virginia before later moving from Edgecombe and Granville counties to create the Lumbee communities.[80] To address the issue of Cherokee cultural appropriation by the Lumbees the tribe claims that the oral and genealogical records show that after the Trail of Tears many Cherokees came into the communities to hide from removal as they had links to the group prior to the event. In a letter from A. W. McLean dated September 7, 1914, to the Department of The Interior, McLean writes on this subject stating, "As will be noted from the historical sketch given by me at the committee hearing hereinbefore mentioned, John Lowrie signed a treaty on the part of the Cherokee Indians with the United States Government in 1806, This John Lowrie was the ancestor of some of the Lowrie Indians now living in Robeson County. His brother, James Lowrie, was one of the most prominent Indians in the county in the year 1810."[81] This shows that there were known historical connections through documented descendants between the Cherokee and the Lumbee Indians even though

---

[80] Cherokee Communities Of The South." *The Melungeon Indians,* historical-melungeons.com/rk_thomas.html.

[81] Partridge, Dennis. "Letter of A.W. McLean in 1914 – Postulating the Origin of the Lumbees." *People of One Fire,* 13 Oct. 2017, peopleofonefire.com/letters_of_a_w_mclean.html.

federally recognized groups, such as the EBCI, deny this fact. As proven by the Lowrie family not only were the Lumbee from Cherokee stock but some of the families had been involved in their political affairs, they even signed treaties as they were in positions of power among the Cherokee people, in the past regarding the United States.

So then why is the modern academic research less valid on the Lumbee tribe according to the federally recognized groups? Is it because the research has been done by non-Natives as insinuated by the Eastern Band of Cherokee Indians? This would hold true if it were not for the fact that most research of the past was done by many non-native people. To include the work done from white Anthropologists like James Mooney, anthropologists that helped to establish the distinct community of the Eastern Band of Cherokee Indians in the first place. My second question would be, why is it that these disenfranchised peoples are viewed as fake Native Americans in the eyes of the public just because the population in discussion is not yet a federally recognized group? The answer to this is that the federal government does not care enough to fully get involved. They let other federally recognized tribes say they are more credible, through action of opinion, about the culture of their historical tribes, while at the same time labeling other non-recognized peoples as fakes because they now have altered practices from each other, totally disregarding the fact that cultures evolve with every migration becoming amalgamated with the other cultures they come into contact with resulting in these multicultural communities in the process; letting these federally recognized groups proclaim their feelings towards the validity of the statements made by other unrecognized groups in court proceedings undermines the sovereignty of the original petitioning party in the first place, as the federal government is initially saying that the historical information provided, by the said group, is all just lies before it is even presented. This is inferred by the fact that there is no federal regulation in place that requires a community to have their genealogy and history scrutinized from a current tribal body, or to even be corroborated by a currently recognized tribe, to show proof of historical connection between any factions of a group, yet federal tribes are allowed to submit their opinions as to the validity of a petitioning group's genealogies, historical documents, and oral histories provided to the BIA. By allowing other recognized tribes to comment to the BIA, the government is, saying they do not believe that the documents that were originally provided are real. This also shows how the process of tribal recognition leans heavily on the opinion of the other federally recognized tribes and not necessarily the historical record as stated in the Federal Acknowledgement Process as a requirement.

As we can see, the federally recognized groups deny the validity of tribal factions by weighing in on the question of "who is Indian?" and by claiming that everyone who does not practice just like them are fakes. The government tends to listen to the federally recognized tribes disregarding the bad blood that may be present among these groups, as seen with the Cherokees, from the past or the fact that other tribal factions may have different cultural practices, as they have become their own separate Indian communities over the years, yet they still claim their historical core names such as Cherokee, as it is a part of their history, like the Lumbee tribe has done in the past. Other tribes should not be able to define the heritage and culture of another based on their long-standing political relationships held with the United States of America.

It seems as if Indian groups like the Eastern Band of Cherokee Indians are relying on the broken system known as the Federal Acknowledgement Process to insure their power and their political status as the only Federally Recognized tribe within their state of North Carolina, reaping benefits like gaming rights, grants, and federal programs reserved only for recognized tribes, such as health care, while making statements like, "decisions about federal acknowledgment of groups as Indian tribes should be based on merit and not politics," while they simultaneously, and hypocritically, lobby with other groups in the affairs of federal politics against all new Acknowledgement of unrecognized Cherokee communities.[82] The Cherokee Nation has continued the Civil War and have engaged in psychological operations to gain control and maintain power since the Coup of the Ross faction as we will go over in the next section; matters of slavery, racism, and political power have been at the center of the Cherokee Civil War since the beginning, and as you will see, the United States government has always been in favor of supporting the National Party, and their form of government, over any other faction of Cherokee.

-----

[82] "Tribe Establishes Cherokee Identity Protection Committee." *The Cherokee One Feather,* 14 Oct. 2011, theonefeather.com/2011/10/tribe-establishes-cherokee-identity-protection-committee/.

PRIDE & PREJUDICE:
Twisting Facts to Maintain a Narrative

One of the worst cases of misinformation in America to date is slavery within the Cherokee Nation. What the Cherokee Nation would like people to believe is that they were disproportionately pro-Union "full bloods", maintained to the long-house culture, and were politically opposed to the "mixed-bloods" who adhered to Southern white cultural norms and belonged to the Knights of the Golden Circle.[83] However, this is blatantly false as I will show using source documents and the words from the Cherokee leaders themselves. First the Cherokee Nation of Old was vastly diverse as we have gone over. There were multiple factions, and to say that the Ross faction leadership had more "full bloods" does not detract from the fact that both factions lived in a mixed society, and that the Old Settlers were in fact the ones hundreds of miles away still living under something that somewhat reflected the traditional Cherokee rule, not the Cherokee Nation of Old that had conformed to a government that reflected that of the United States. By the 1780s U.S. officials had started to usher the Cherokees away from hunting and their traditional ways of life, and to instead learn how to live, worship, and farm like Christian American yeomen. Because of this, the Cherokees went on the have factional divides among the nation as it negotiated its assimilation with the more traditional groups becoming secluded from the politics or leaving to other lands. During this assimilation process the Cherokee Nation of Old established a court system, formally abandoned the law of

---

[83] "Pin Indians: The Encyclopedia of Oklahoma History and Culture." *Pin Indians | The Encyclopedia of Oklahoma History and Culture*, https://www.okhistory.org/publications/enc/entry.php?entry=PI008.

blood revenge, and adopted a republican government.[84] So the reality is the Cherokee Nation is splitting hairs when making these blood quantum-based arguments of what party was "full bloods" or "mixed bloods" as the fact is the state of the Nation for the Cherokee Confederacy was more so broken down in the following by the 1830s:

1. The Cherokee Nation of Old in the East decided to support assimilation to the Southern society's way of life, and thus underwent assimilation into mass American culture to achieve such ends, becoming mixed bloods of various degrees as the intermarriage practice with whites became common, to retain lands as the years went on and excursions began.

2. The Western Cherokees, or the Cherokee Nation "West," who were disproportionately full bloods, avoided many aspects of assimilation, and removed to lands west of the Mississippi River, to retain their tribal identity and form of traditional government by factional rule.

3. Both the Ross and Ridge parties represented mixed blood factions however, but still the Cherokee Nation makes it a point to say that the Ross party had more "full bloods" even though it holds no relevance when looking at the matters at hand, as the Ridge Party had an alliance with the Western Cherokees who were by all accounts the "full bloods" and traditional Cherokee People; while the National Party, or Ross faction as they are better known, represented a newly established Cherokee government based on western societies rule of the lands in many aspects of life.

This speak by the Cherokee Nation historians, and thus fellow scholars, to the amount of Cherokee blood is done only to try to undercut and discredit the Treaty Party. Many full bloods

---

[84] *Cherokee Removal - New Georgia Encyclopedia.* https://www.georgiaencyclopedia.org/articles/history-archaeology/cherokee-removal/.

were educated in the ways of the white society, and obtained the same schooling as those in the Ridge group, were in the Ross faction as well so the talk of "mixed bloods" is done so to make the Ridge faction sound as if though they are less Indian, which is false; and thus, had less of a right to make decisions about tribal matters on behalf of the Nation. While I while agree the gun was jumped with the signing of the 1835 Treaty, as there was not a full consensus in the Cherokee Nation of Old between the two leading factions to decide either way, this does not mean that the Treaty Party did not have authority within the tribal body, because they did. The Cherokee Nation and historians often speak to them as the Minority Party who usurped power to sell out the Cherokee Nation "East" of their ancestral homelands.[85] While that argument can be made, that is if you only look at the group as representative of the faction still living in the Cherokee Nation of Old.

However, The Treaty Party were aligned with the full blood, traditional factions found in the Cherokee Nation "West", as we have covered, who advocated that the Cherokee Nation of Old, or Cherokee Nation "East" as it was known to by the US Federal government, be reunited with them west of the Mississippi to help rebuild the once great nation. Now it is important to note that these two groups were but part of the Cherokee Confederacy that was operational in the 1830s, but at the time these two had the biggest governments with government-to-government relationships with the USA, however other factions were well known to the United States as well, like Chief Bowls group of Texas Cherokee found in Rusk and Cherokee Counties, in East Texas.[86] When you consider this, then the Ross Party was actually

---

[85] Magazine, Smithsonian. "The Treaty That Forced the Cherokee People from Their Homelands Goes on View." *Smithsonian.com*, Smithsonian Institution, 24 Apr. 2019, https://www.smithsonianmag.com/blogs/national-museum-american-indian/2019/04/24/treaty-new-echota/.

[86] Smith, Emily. "Sam Houston & Chief Bowl (Duwali) (Aka 'the Treaty')." *East Texas History*, https://easttexashistory.org/items/show/310.

the minority faction in the greater scheme of things. However, the Ross Party felt that the Eastern and Western Cherokee had become two different entities, as they believed their society was more advantageous[87], as their elites had become accustomed to the practices of Southern culture such as slavery, a Republican form of government, and a court system that mimicked that of the United States South-eastern Southern States, and thus should not have to regroup with the Western Cherokee as they were the "Civilized Tribe" while the Western Cherokee still held on to old forms of Cherokee law.[88]

In every case, wording matters, and the Cherokee Nation has used phrasing to blur lines in the present to lead campaigns aimed at the historical eraser of other Cherokee factions, and to make issues of the past murky to their own benefit. Such is the case with slavery within the Cherokee Nation. The truth is the Cherokee Nation as a whole supported the Southern cause to start with, for the first time since the Treaty of New Echota, the leaders of both the Ross, Ridge, and the Western Cherokee factions all found themselves on the same page, as the Cherokee Confederacy had only had broken Treaties with the Federal government up until that point and saw an opportunity by aligning with the Southern States to regain a more traditional form of government as Indian City-states of Arkansas and Oklahoma that would operate more in the fashion of the Cherokee government of old, with the power more distributed to the towns as a representative democratic electorates within the states. It was only when the tides of War started to shift that the "loyal Cherokee", those who were known as the Ross faction but now having served for the Union had taken to calling themselves the "Loyal Cherokee", and the founders of what would ultimately become the Cherokee Nation, would split away from the South to join

---

[87] Ratified treaty no. 358, documents relating to the negotiation of the treaty of July 19, 1866, with the Cherokee Indians (July 19,1866)
[88] Ibid.

the Union. They did this because the Cherokee leaders had a split in the tribe. Half the tribe wanted to stay with the South to ensure that Arkansas and Oklahoma would become Indian States to be governed by indigenous laws,[89] such as no slavery or personal land ownership, while the ones who defected to the North only did so because they were promised that they would be allowed to keep their slaves, those who would become the Cherokee Freedmen, in Indian Territory because it technically was not a state. As it was put by one historian, "native peoples understood freedom as the watchword of U.S. imperialism; their defense of tribal sovereignty converged with the vindication of slavery and its segregationist legacy."[90]

In Transcriptions from the Pre-Treaty Negotiations of the Cherokee Treaty of 1866 we can see that the Ross faction can attest to this. In this Interview between the Chiefs and the Headmen of the Cherokee Nation, with the Ross Party, or the group now being referred to as "Loyal Cherokee", represented by Mr. Ewing, and the Southern Cherokee, this was the Cherokees who stayed Confederate aligned throughout the duration of the war, and who's leaders were from the Treaty Party and Western Cherokees in the past, represented by Mr. Voorhees. The meeting was moderated by the Hon. D. W. Cooley, Commissioner of Indian Affairs, and Indian Superintendent Sells, at the office of Indian Affairs, March 30th, 1866. So, in this discussion, written in the minutes in black and white, we can see that the Pro-Union, or "Pin Indians", were the true supporters of the slavery cause. With the man standing in defense of the "Loyal Cherokee" himself, Mr. Ewing, stating out right in the discussion that, "the knights of the golden circle were peppered by the 'pin society'

---

[89] Ibid.

[90] Saunt, Claudio. "The Paradox of Freedom: Tribal Sovereignty and Emancipation during the Reconstruction of Indian Territory." *The Journal of Southern History*, vol. 70, no. 1, Southern Historical Association, 2004, pp. 63–94, https://doi.org/10.2307/27648312.

of the Loyal Cherokee".[91] The Cherokee Nation likes to frame it as if the Kee-too-wah were a continuous strong influence in the Nation for 200 years prior to the 1830s. However, this group was not a continuous fixture of political influence, as their numbers both grew, and waned, depending on the times, and thus they did not always have the sway the Cherokee Nation would like us to believe they had.

Historian Edward Dale talked on the topic of the Kee-too-wah stating, "In addition to the factions mentioned, the Cherokees, like most other Indian tribes, tended to divide into two groups. These were the conservatives, who clung closely to the old Indian customs and way of life, and the progressives, who hoped to advance their people in civilization and induce them to follow, at least in some measure, the white man's road. The conservative group, composed largely of full-bloods, in 1859 revived an ancient organization known as the Kee-too-wah, taking as their insignia two common pins worn in the form of a cross."[92] In order for something to be revived it has to have waned in support over time, as the group had lost support over the years since its highest point in 1838. He goes on to say, "in consequence, members of the order were commonly called 'Pins.' These were intensely loyal to Chief Ross who, although a large slaveholder, continued to retain the confidence of the full-blood element. The progressive division of the Cherokees soon formed chapters of the Copperhead organization, the Knights of the Golden Circle, and looked to Stand Watie for leadership."[93] So, unlike the rest of the war, the situation was flipped for the Cherokee in were the Confederate Cherokee fought for freedom, as in the right to

---

[91] Ibid.

[92] Dale, Edward Everett. "The Cherokees in the Confederacy." The Journal of Southern History, vol. 13, no. 2, Southern Historical Association, 1947, pp. 159–85, https://doi.org/10.2307/2197976.

[93] Ibid.

go back to the old ways of governmental rule of the Cherokee;[94] while the Union bunch fought for slavery, and their now modern form of government, as well as to be the authority within Indian country absorbing in smaller tribes into their fold stripping them of their perspective individual autonomies.[95]

For those that do not know, the knights of the golden circle were a secret society founded in 1854 by American George W. L. Bickley, the objective of which was to create a new country, known as the Golden Circle, where slavery would be legal. This shows how the Union Cherokee were whole heartedly in bed with slavery up until the end of the war, in where they still made strides to inforce degrees of it through segregationist actions as formerly mentioned. Mr. Voorhees goes on to make this point by stating the hypocrisies saying to Ewing, "The only names on several documents leading the Cherokee Nation into rebellion and the man Mr. Ewing referenced, John Ross says he represents the Cherokee Nation. We were [led] into the rebellion by men who are represented by Mr. E. The only difference is that they were false to two Gov'ts. And we were false to only one. The Ross party left when success was waning.".[96] The United States also knew they, in not so many words, were indicating that they were going to let slavery exist in Indian Territory as the tribes were currently Sovereign government with rule over their own lands, as well to get the Ross party to change sides, and as such, tried not to discuss the matter in the document with Mr. Cooley stating in his closing remarks that, "I would like this question left out, about the societies 'pin' and 'Golden Circle'."[97]

---

[94] Tindle, James Franklin. "'Perpetual Peace and Friendship': The Cherokee-Confederate Coalition in the American Civil War." *K*, 1 Jan. 1970, https://krex.k-state.edu/dspace/handle/2097/39814.

[95] Ratified treaty no. 358, documents relating to the negotiation of the treaty of July 19, 1866, with the Cherokee Indians (July 19,1866)

[96] Ibid.

[97] Ibid.

Now days when you go to what are believed to be reputable sources to get summarized accounts of history, as that is how most interact with the past in modern times, they do not give any insight to the real history that happen and often blatantly lie on the facts. Case and point, if you look up, "what are the Pin Indians?", on Google your first hit will be the Oklahoma Historical Society. Their definition of the term is that "The derogatory term 'Pin Indians' was applied by Treaty Party Cherokees to hostile, pro-Union Cherokee, Creek, and Seminole during the Civil War. The Pins were identified by cross pins worn on their coat lapels or calico shirts. They were disproportionately full bloods, wore turbans, adhered to the long-house culture, and were politically opposed to the frock-coated mixed-bloods who adhered to Southern white cultural norms and belonged to the Knights of the Golden Circle." However, as the source documents show, this is a lie. The Pins where the ones in bed with the Golden Knights, and the Union Cherokees would have loved to continue slavery post-Civil War if given the opportunity, as seen in the lack of accountability and documentation put forth towards the freedmen faction during the Dawes process, and their subsequent treatment thereafter.

During this same Treaty negotiation, the Ross Party showed its cards, as it had ambitions of being something larger and more powerful moving forward than what it was at the time, as it had to share its power with other factions of Cherokee in the past, laying out the case that the Loyal Cherokee, and the Cherokee Nation they had built, was now too big to fail. Ewing argued that since the 1830s the Ross and Ridge Parties had been at odds, with the Ridge Party requesting that they be considered a sovereign tribal body from the Ross faction altogether, and that since the government had supported the Ross faction so far, turning down the request of the Treaty Party in the past, then they must continue to follow suit to ensure that the biggest tribe in Indian Territory could be seen as a beacon of how a Indian nation can move from "savages" to "Civilized" under the tutorship of the United States government with Mr. Ewing stating:

> Down to 1846 the Stand Watie Party had been demanding a division. The General Gov't. refused to allow it. If it is done now, it will be nothing but a premium for disloyalty. It must be so regarded by the Cherokees who have been true to the Gov't and who will never consent to the division of the nation. Mr. V. says they have distracted and torn. The nation and the government should be worried with the effort to retain the Unity of the Cherokee Nation. Let him point to an Indian tribe from the Lakes to the Pacific that has been so wisely governed as them. Common schools, churches, seminaries, well-filled, -Cove the country, and they have a gov't more just and firmer than any gov't of whites on the frontier. The Cherokee Gov't has been a great achievement for the Indians and a oneness of the Gen'l Gov't in its policy towards them.

It should be stated that the Cherokee Nation has performed the function of a puppet government after the Civil War within Indian Territory, for the guise of progress among the Indian for the United States government, but this balance was struck deliberately by the elites in the Ross faction to ensure political dominance over all other factions of Cherokee in terms of government-to-government relationships with the USA during the Treaty of 1867. However, the Ross Party, in full awareness of all agreements made in the Treaty of 1867, never upheld the terms within the Cherokee Nation, the US government never made an attempt to write this matter, and thus, these so called "Loyal Cherokee" started to participate in the segregationist actions of Jim Crow in the Cherokee Nation post construction; it wasn't until 2017 that the freedmen faction was allowed to enroll in the tribe, although they have yet to have received any real help to date from the Cherokee Nation. But yet when black history month comes around the Cherokee Nation is quick to ask for the stories of this muted people of color, tri-racial isolate community, that they were forced by the courts to include in their Nation, to act as if they care, as if it isn't a show for others, while not providing actual benefits to the faction itself.[98] Showing once more how the Cherokee Nation even today wishes to display a picture of inclusivity of support for all its factions, however, as we know that is not the case, as history has proven. With noted leaders such as Wilma Mankiller, dubiously spearheading efforts to force the disenfranchisement of other Cherokee factions of multi racial peoples, like when she signed multiple resolutions to bar the Freedmen descendants from citizenship during her tenure,[99] while later writing in her autobiography the following words, "The truth is that the practice of slavery will forever cast a shadow on the great Cherokee Nation",[100] as she committed racist acts herself as principle Chief at the expense of African American Cherokee Citizens within the Nation. The tribe notoriously puts out the image of inclusivity while behind the scenes they do everything they can to maintain the status quo of the Cherokee Nation's superior status as gatekeepers, and as economic & political power houses; and as we can see, sadly, they are teaching this practice to other Cherokee factions as well in other parts of America.

---

[98] Grajeda, Antoinette, et al. "Cherokee Nation Seeks Cherokee Freedmen Stories, Photographs." *Arkansas Soul | Black and Minority News in Arkansas*, 4 Feb. 2022, https://argotsoul.com/2022/02/cherokee-nation-seeks-cherokee-freedmen-stories-photographs/.

[99] "The Cherokee Nation Must Be Free to Expel Black Freedmen | James Mackay." *The Guardian*, Guardian News and Media, 17 Sept. 2011, https://www.theguardian.com/commentisfree/2011/sep/17/cherokee-nation-black-freedmen.

[100] Daffron, Brian. "Citizenship Denied: The Latest in the Cherokee Freedmen Saga." *Indian Country Today*, Indian Country Today, 9 Sept. 2011, https://indiancountrytoday.com/archive/citizenship-denied-the-latest-in-the-cherokee-freedmen-saga.

Official Seal of the Group

THE SOUTHERN CHEROKEE INDIAN TRIBE:

Story of Erasure, Historical Gas Lighting, The Oppression of a Peoples

To not repeat historical facts, and with no disrespect for the history of the Southern Cherokee, I would like to not dive too deep into the beginnings of the Cherokee Civil War, as the Southern Cherokee Tribe does have its own rich heritage, this should not be understated, but in an effort to keep things easily digestible we will keep it short by focusing on the time frame around the latter half of the 1800s, where the group left the main body of the tribe in Oklahoma in 1867.

A general overview of the group in present day would tell us that the Southern Cherokee, also known as The Treaty Tribe, has members that span across the Ozarks, and like any other tribal body, it also has peoples that can be found in other places around the United States as well, although to a much lesser extent. However, as just stated, most of these families currently live in the Ozarks and around its surrounding areas, with the core of the tribe living in Phelps County, Missouri. The Southern Cherokee Indian Tribe has 527 enrolled members that claim their heritage back to the Cherokee Nation of Old before the removals period.[101] The people have held strong bonds to each other throughout the years regardless to the hardship and oppression they faced. These people still live rural lifestyles that often consist of farming, hunting, and fishing to sustain. Some of the people work modern jobs within towns and cities but most families are farmers who freely share goods and etcetera whenever the need arises within the community.[102] The median income for a household of four for this tribe is roughly $15,000 a year with most of the peoples working minimum wage and odd jobs for ends meet, while others can't work due to poor health, with only a very small number of the tribal members owning small businesses within the area. The estimated high school graduation rate for the Southern Cherokee is 50% with college graduates being almost nonexistent.[103] If we go back and reexamine Cherokee history we can see just when and where the Southern Cherokee became lost to the winds regarding the greater tribal body in Oklahoma, as it was not that long ago when it happened.

The Southern Cherokee became separated completely from the faction that would become the base of the Cherokee tribe in Oklahoma after the Civil War. The reason the Southern Cherokee sided with the south was because the Cherokee blood law had made the Southern Cherokee targets within the nation since the Trail of Tears leading to the assassination of many of their

---

[101] Matthews, Darla Gene. "The Southern Cherokee Indian Tribe Tsalagi Tsuganwv (Also Known as the Treaty Tribe)." Missouri, United States, Newburg , 30 Apr. 2015, 92.

[102] Ibid., 2.

[103] Ibid., 93.

leaders. This fracture in the nation caused a lot of Cherokee to find refuge in Arkansas and Missouri, as they had once settled there before the Removals, and many Old Settlers remained in the area at the time, as after the removals they refused to move into Indian Territory during the Trail of Tears. Some prominent figures within the Southern Cherokee who migrated back to these areas were Elias Boudinot and Stand Watie. Both families lived in the state of Arkansas by the 1850s. During the Civil War, these migrations of Cherokee out of Indian Territory were so severe that the whites in Northwest Arkansas started to call for the removal of the more abrasive and aggressive Indians from the state.[104]

Prior to the Anglo settlement of the Southeastern states the Cherokees were once a great confederacy. This confederacy was made up of all different regional tribal groups, as we have gone over prior, such as the Cherokee Nation "East," "West," and the multitude of political entities within them from the Pins to the Old Settlers, Ross Faction, and Treaty Party aligned peoples, which were united by culture, religion, and language. But to recap the subject once more so the gravity is understood, after years of their land being systematically taken from them by the United States of America, through countless broken treaties, the leadership within the Cherokee Confederacy started to view the situation of assimilation in different lights than each other. This caused division among the tribal factions. It came to an apex for the Southern Cherokee after the removals that were ushered in by the Treaty of New Echota, in 1838, which was the cause for the Cherokee peoples in the East being removed to Oklahoma Territory. The United States of America knew in the mid-1800s that the Cherokee were peoples were a divided people, however, at the expense of the other factions of Cherokee

---

[104] SMITHERS, GREGORY D. CHEROKEE DIASPORA: an Indigenous History of Migration, Resettlement, and Identity. (YALE UNIVERSITY PRESS, 2018), 137.

within their Confederacy the United States never resolved the issues.

We know this because in 1846, the Cherokees were already viewed by members of the U.S. Congress and President James K. Polk as a tribe that had formed deep splits between their leadership. This is highlighted in a special message to Congress written by then President Polk in which he stated, "In my annual message of the 2nd of December last it was stated that serious difficulties of long standing continued to distract the several parties into which the Cherokee tribe of Indians is unhappily divided; that all the efforts of the Government to adjust these difficulties had proved to be unsuccessful, and would probably remain so without the aid of further legislation by Congress. Subsequent events have confirmed this opinion."[105] The internal disputes between the now Southern Cherokee families and the greater body of tribal peoples identified as the Cherokee Nation of Oklahoma started back east before the removals, and continued into the west, ending with the division of the once great nation into multiple groups. Most notably the Oklahoma Cherokees and subsequently smaller tribes and bands that settled across the Ozarks. The Southern Cherokee's main body of members was in the past, and is currently, made up of families who sided with the confederacy during the Civil War. The tribal members can often cite their ancestors who fought with the South on their base roll, which is the Tompkins Roll.

After the Civil War, by 1873, there began to be three groups in Oklahoma that started to form in the Cherokee Nation. These groups were the "full bloods, mixed bloods, and Negroes"[106] and considerable fighting broke out amongst the groups. The Southern Cherokee Indian Tribe decided to leave Oklahoma and

---

[105] Matthews, Darla Gene. "The Southern Cherokee Indian Tribe Tsalagi Tsuganwv (Also Known as the Treaty Tribe)." Missouri, United States, Newburg , 30 Apr. 2015, 1.
[106] Ibid., 82.

move back to Missouri. This was during the Jim Crow Era and as a result the Southern Cherokee decided to stay secluded to protect their peoples. The reason given for the tribe's relocation is best described by D.M. Cooley:

> I have insisted on a separation, into two bands, of the Cherokees. I have for another purpose, in this report, mentioned the ancient feud of the Cherokees. That feud still exists … and that it has always existed since it first arose there can be no doubt. At different periods of Cherokee history, it has shown itself. Nearly every distinguished man of the Ridge party has been killed, and Ridge himself, 28 years ago, fell by the assassin's knife, while many of a lesser note on both sides, growing out of this Ross And Ridge feud, have died with violence. The ridge party join the rebellion, and with their families went South, where they mostly now are. The Ross party say they will forgive them, reinstate them in their homes and afford them protection to life, liberty, and prosperity, but they must come back and submit to their jurisdiction. The Ridge party say that their offense is against the United States, and not against the Cherokee Nation, which has no right to talk of forgiveness; they have no confidence in the promises of the Ross party, or any other they may make; they say they have trusted them before, and been deceived. That they are afraid of assassination and depredations on their liberty and property, but more afraid of judicial murderers, robberies and deprivations of liberty, than from open assault; and say they never can and never will try to live with the Ross party until there is a decided change, of which they say they can as yet see no signs.[107]

After attacks on the Southern Cherokee peoples continued, they felt it necessary to cut ties and head out to Missouri.

------

[107] Ibid., 84.

Even after leaving Oklahoma the tribe still held their heritage and history as the base of which criteria for enrollment is proven. One must prove their descendants from an ancestor that was with Stand Watie's Mounted Rifles, or from a person that is listed on the Tompkins Roll of 1867, which listed Cherokees living in the Canadian or Kooweeskoowee Districts of then Indian Territory. A person must trace their genetic lines back to the mounted rifles, then that person must also be involved in the functions of the Southern Cherokee Community, to be eligible for enrollment into the tribe.[108] In other words it is not just enough to have the blood of the Southern Cherokee in the past; but one must also be active within the community itself to be eligible to be a member. The Southern Cherokee Indian Tribe peoples of the present day relate to their ancestors of the past through their genealogies to historical rolls and their current land links. In present time the tribe defines their members by relying on their community involvement to define the group beyond just their blood of the past. Their tribal body is taking a different approach to enrollment relying not on their blood quantum to define who is a Southern Cherokee but a person's community connection to the group as it exists now. Missouri and Arkansas are where the Southern Cherokee are where the tribe calls home, with some still residing in Oklahoma, and the nucleus of the Tribal body being in Missouri. With the lands in Southern Cherokee Communities possessing a regional dialect only found within the Ozarks; as the Southern Cherokee have specifically created their own sub dialect in this area, as mentioned in the past, they still speak English, but they utilize terms in different ways due to the sociolinguistic evolution of their culture.

There are many Native cultures that have lost their language in the past but also managed to have utilized English in a different way than those around them. This is in part because they learned English as a second language in the past and thus, they

---

[108] "Enrollment Criteria." *Southern Cherokee Indian Tribe,* thesoutherncherokee.org/tribal-enrollment/.

created their own communal dialects over the course of generations. This can be seen in the Ozarks as well as in the tribe's original homelands like Virginia and North Carolina. One example of the variation in speech patterns of English, and the use of its words to mean something different than their original meaning, can be seen when looking at Lumbee culture, as prior stated, and the use of their regional dialect. The Lumbee use words such as Ellick, Juvember, Mommuck, Toten, or Mum,[109] in their daily speech that is considered outside of the norm for average Americans. Much like native communities in the Ozarks the Lumbee's sociolinguistics developed around the English language while also identifying the peoples as separate entities in the same process. The Southern Cherokee have their own dialect, which is still in current use, which evolved in their seclusion.

So, then the question is raised, how did the southern Cherokee end up in Missouri? The Southern Cherokee have some members who share roots with the Chickamauga communities, aka Old Settlers or Western Cherokee, as the Treaty Party was aligned with the Cherokee Nation "West" and as such, within the Southern Cherokee's petition to the BIA they address this matter further:

> Missouri housed rich hunting grounds that the Cherokee and other tribes had frequented since before the Europeans stepped on the shores of America. The lush surroundings caused some to remain. As pressure was exerted on those southern Cherokee living west of the Mississippi, the number who migrated here increased. In fact, Cherokee people had in habited Missouri since the signing of the 1793 treaty with Spain, prior to that date there was a treaty with France. Via a Royal proclamation, France once again bought the land back from Spain, along with other lands, 'tracked after tract.' To prove geographical context, when France

---

[109] "Indian by Birth: The Lumbee Dialect." *YouTube.com,* m.youtube.com/playlist?list=PL-raHaHvF0UezcisJ861V9SNgkD7SKr_k.

bought the land from Spain, Missouri was a part of the Louisiana purchase. The United States agreed to protect Native Americans as stated in the treaty, of which the Cherokee was one. It should be pointed out that the promised protection was never forthcoming. Over the years, many southern Cherokee migrated to Southern Missouri below the St. Francis River, during the Trail of Tears, as did members of other tribes. It was in Central Missouri that the majority of southern Cherokee settled after the initial treaty with Spain. To reiterate, having some other people already in Missouri was one of the primary reasons that the Southern Cherokee relocated here from Oklahoma after the U.S. Civil War. It was also where the Ridges lived for a time, along with many of the Southern Cherokee/Treaty party. So, it was the logical place the Southern Cherokee would migrate to when it was necessary to leave Oklahoma.[110]

The Southern Cherokee were also faced with displacement in the 20th century, in the same way that the Saponi in Missouri did for the creation of the national parks, with the construction of Fort Leonard Wood in the 1940s. Some of their villages were located within, and subsequently move from, the bounds of the then proposed Post that currently encompasses more than 61,000 acres. This happened as the U.S. Government used their right of eminent domain to acquire much of the land to build Fort Leonard Wood; a practice which has been done time and time again at the expense of the populations within these areas of Missouri.[111] The residents of many small towns and villages

---

[110] Matthews, Darla Gene. "The Southern Cherokee Indian Tribe Tsalagi Tsuganwv (Also Known as the Treaty Tribe)." Missouri, United States, Newburg, 30 Apr. 2015, 84, 85.

[111] Nicklaus, David. "The Long, Sad History of Eminent Domain in Missouri." *Stltoday.com,* 18 Oct. 2007, www.stltoday.com/business/columns/david-nicklaus/the-long-sad-history-of-eminent-domain-in-missouri/article_0c5ede20-dabb-5414-ae22-bae44a51cde9.html.

were forced to move from their homes to make way for this new post leaving their homes for what was often pennies on the dollar for their lands. The most notable of those forced to move were that of the residents of the town by the name of Bloodland which was heavily populated with Southern Cherokees. One of the families that was affected by the building of the Post, in where the family was forced to move from Bloodland to other parts of the Ozarks, were the Gray family. This is the family from whom the Southern Cherokee Indian Tribe's Council member Johnny Gray descends from.

Bloodland and these other crossroad settlements had survived in the hills untouched from the late 1800s on. To quote the southern Cherokee, "having to remain sequestered in the forest was the main deterrent to success. It impacted every aspect of southern Cherokee life. The fear of sending children to school virtually stop the progress within the tribe. As the world around us changed, grew matured, the world for the Southern Cherokee remained unchanged. "[112] But regardless to this, it was their safe spot for decades, and where they had raised families. It was these families' homes, and they loved them in lieu of the dark circumstances of how they got there. Another storm came for the family groups affected, and the Southern Cherokee as a whole, on October 31, 1940, when it was announced that communities were scheduled to be demolished by the United States Government. By 1943, four towns and a few smaller settlements sprinkled along old Missouri Hwy. 17 were destroyed to make way for barracks and training areas of Fort Leonard Wood, leaving only the 15 cemeteries on the Army Post to attest to their existence.[113] While some families were compensated for the force move, it

---

[112] Matthews, Darla Gene. "The Southern Cherokee Indian Tribe Tsalagi Tsuganwv (Also Known as the Treaty Tribe)." Missouri, United States, Newburg, 30 Apr. 2015, 93.

[113] Miller, Tom. "GRAVES STAND AS REMINDER OF LOST TOWNS." *Chicagotribune.com*, 3 Sept. 2018, www.chicagotribune.com/news/ct-xpm-1987-05-25-8702080343-story.html.

wasn't at value as the Army often times doesn't even pay the cost value for land, and it doesn't make it any less troubling for the people involved; the community was forced with the ultimatum of moving once move, as just like in the 1835 Treaty, they could move with some compensation or be forced to later under gunpoint; however, it might not be the few towns that half to move but the Southern Cherokee that would once more be moved off their lands to a death sentence in Oklahoma, or elsewhere as people of color in the Jim Crow South. This was just one of many forced removals they had experienced, and it has had a dramatic impact on the Southern Cherokee. The effects of the Historical Traumas that have been inflicted on the group, much like the people of the Saponi Nation in Missouri, have made their descendants scared of removals until the current day.

Often, I hear of how people from the older generations, if asked to give an age range I would say those that were born in the 1960s and prior, do not want to be included in my research due to the fears that they hold towards outsiders. Numerous times I have tried to meet with Elders to conduct research only to be told that the person does not want to be involved anymore as they do not trust that they will have anonymity. This distrust towards the outside communities I feel is still present due to the experiences their ancestors faced, and the horror stories that have been passed down through the generations, as my family has some stories about that time that are heart breaking as well. Although I have no affiliation with any government organization other than being a veteran of a foreign war, which is common in indigenous communities to include the Southern Cherokee, I am a Cherokee myself, an enrolled tribal member of an Indian Nation, I am also married to an enrolled Tribal member of the Winnebago Tribe of Nebraska, I am still met with fear by elders of the community because the folk feel that speaking with me will put them on the governments radar exposing them to the possibility of being removed from their lands; even though the young generation seems to be getting away from this way of thought it is still prevalent with many, although the leadership is always willing to make the case for their peoples.

The repeated theme that shows up again and again in the Southern Cherokee Indian Tribe, as well as in other Ozark Indian enclaves, is that of vehemently denying their heritage in the past. This is not to mean that they did not have heritage as discussed in prior sections, but that their culture was sustained in private, as one's heritage being exposed could bring dire consequences for the whole family as people of color during segregation. It is important to let the people speak on their own behalf for why this was. This is vital to understanding their perspective, as every Community is different and has their own unique circumstances for how they got to where they are today:

Upon arrival, the southern Cherokee found that the culture in Missouri was not friendly to Indians. Some of the laws reflected that attitude. The climate within the state of Missouri was incendiary in the early 1830s and beyond. The Mormon population was growing exponentially. Native Americans were not just passing through. They were settling here. Missourians were being bombarded with a religion that was unfamiliar to them; not to mention barbarous Native Americans... Violence began to erupt. A generalized fear served as the stimulus for Missouri residence to hate both the Mormons and Native Americans. It did not help that the southern Cherokee took pity on the Mormons and offer them food and lodging when they were in desperate straits.

That fear is reflected in correspondence to Governor Lilburn Boggs from Daniel Ashby, James Keyte and Sterling Price on September 1, 1835, '… concerning the hostile intentions of the Mormons and their allies, as it is currently reported and believe that they have integrated themselves with the Indians, and they say so, to assist them in there diabolical career' … ' I distinctly recollect hearing Joseph Smith, the prophet, state in a public discourse that he had 14,000 men, not belonging to the church, ready moment's warning which was generally understood to be Indians' … ' we have the best authority for believing that, in their public teachings, there people are taught to believe and expect that immense numbers of Indians ... are only waiting for the signal for a general rise, when, as they stayed it, the 'Flying or Destroying Angel,' will go through the land and work the general destruction of all that are not Mormons.'

On October 27, 1838, Governor Liburn Boggs responded to the fear and signed into law the 'Mormon Extermination Order.' He ordered the Mormon expelled from the state, or 'exterminated,' if necessary. The 'letter of the law' was bad enough. But the 'spirit of the law' was even more diabolical. Both Missouri residents and lawmakers chose to include the southern Cherokee within the purview of the Mormon law. It was well known that not only Mormons could be shot on sight; but our people could also be killed with little provocation. The Mormon law provided the perfect target for hatred and uneasiness. First emotions were directed towards the Mormons; then on to the Southern Cherokee.

Unfortunately, the dissension within the state of Missouri did not improve much. The state was a microcosm for both the Civil War and post war attitudes. Not only was the state divided on whether to support the North or South; but many families were torn apart by the same war, organizations of veterans of the North and South were formed, fueling the continued animosity. Northern veterans join the grand Army of the Republic and Confederate veterans enrolled in the United Confederate Veterans. For many years, G.A.R. Posts and U.C.V. Chapters met over reunion campfires retelling stories and recalling the friends who did not return. The G.A.R. and U.C.V. held powerful influence in political circles from 1878 through the turn of the century.

These kinds of formalized activities kept the dissidence alive. Both Missouri and Arkansas saw the emergence of guerilla violence in the postwar years. To add to the mix, outlaw Jesse James became the face of postwar violence. Residents were looking for a scapegoat and for people to blame for their troubles. Despite the protection that was promised to the Southern Cherokee by the 1866 treaty, safety was an elusive luxury.

For their own protection, the Southern Cherokee had become accustomed to meeting in family groups and clans. Several of the southern Cherokee can still remember when these family gatherings began to, once again, become more serious, I.E. Southern Cherokee meetings on May 27, 1899. Some of the meeting places included Kenneth Allen farm, swinging Bridge, big Springs and blooms garden. Blooms garden is a place that is held to be holy, Sacred among the southern Cherokee; not just because of the meeting that took place there, but also because of the fact that several southern Cherokee Headmen and Beloved Women were buried there. This is a Sacred Cherokee culture that has been traditionally carried through the years, and yet today the burial site is considered to be public. In fact, there also are several Missourians buried there with the southern Cherokee. This is such affront. But again, fear has prevented these wrongs from being rectified; nor has the many promises been fulfilled by the United States.[114]

In the 1900s, the southern Cherokee kept records of their dealings by transcribing in their journals and letters what had been discussed as important business at their annual meetings. These recordings in their journals were often cryptic messages of the ongoing fear the Southern Cherokee experienced in Missouri. Also recorded within these annals are the accounts of squabbles that occurred within the families and other concerns raised between each other within the group.[115] The southern Cherokee have been visible, and fighting within the courts, for over 40 years now and still have not been recognized by the state or federal government with the rights they deserve true the trust doctrine as they once were in the past.

----

[114] Matthews, Darla Gene. "The Southern Cherokee Indian Tribe Tsalagi Tsuganwv (Also Known as the Treaty Tribe)." Missouri, United States, Newburg, 30 Apr. 2015, 85, 86.
[115] Ibid., 87.

UNRECOGNIZED STRUGGLES

Lack of formal teaching on the subject in schools has left a false understanding of what, how, and why an Indigenous nation practices their cultures, as well as allowed for a situation in where the history of Indigenous groups has been curated for political power in a way the manipulates the past to serve the means of the elites of a tribal body. When people think of Native Americans, sadly, they expect stereotypes. They often believe that the cultures are stuck in the 19th century. I can make the claim that all Native Americans have experienced some form of a shift in cultural identity within their history since they have had contact with Anglo-settlers. Whether the change was from nomadic societies to agrarian communities the people adapt to the situation at hand. Tribal lands across the United States of America have been merged and thus separate tribes have united into one governing body in the present day such as the Mandan, Hidatsa, and Arikara Nation located in North Dakota, the Confederated Tribes of Coos, Lower Umpqua and Siuslaw Indians, or the Confederated Tribes of the Grand Ronde Community of Oregon, that consists of twenty-seven tribes that come together as one government. In the past other indigenous factions were made almost subservient to the bigger tribes in the areas where they were placed in Indian Territory as I have gone over with the second Coup of the Cherokee Nation in 1867. But for an example of the impact this had we can look to the Delaware. It was not until 2008 that the Delaware, headquartered in Bartlesville, Oklahoma was able to sign a memorandum of agreement that allowed them to start to try at regaining their rights to sovereignty through federal recognition breaking free from the Cherokee Nation's jurisdiction. So to let this fully sink in, under the force of the federal government, they were placed under this leadership in 1867 and it took them, as recognized people that were subordinate to a greater tribal body's power, almost 140 years to even have its day in the courts to have its rights as a separate tribe and culture, which they are, due to bad politicking of the past done on the part of the United States in an effort to reform Indian Nations into smaller governments reminiscent of their own, led by the Ross Party, in a bid for control of the Cherokee Nation post-Civil War, putting forth a "to big to fail" strategy in the 1866 pre-negotiations Treaty of 1867 discussions as discussed earlier.

Groups adapt as multiple cultures clash on new lands resulting in altered or new traditions, beliefs, and practices as new groups form out of the old. In a lot of cases the new groups continued as new tribes not recognized formally from the United States government resulting in our current situation where "Less than half of self-identified American Indians are registered with a federally recognized tribe, according to the BIA's 2005 American Indian Population and Labor report." And thus, more than half of the self-identified Indians do not get the rights or have the same respect given to them that other federally recognized Native Americans receive. "Federally unrecognized tribes do not have access to the same economic or educational benefits federally recognized ones do, they do not have the same authority over their cultural artifacts or land, nor do they hold the same political weight,"[116] and as a result the folk are caught in a cycle of oppression of their cultures.

The oppression of Unrecognized Tribes trough the political means is nothing new. Since the Civil Rights movement, this issue has been present. In 1977, at the request of the Federal government, a Commission of Native Americans pointed the problem out stating, "From the viewpoint of tribes seeking to clarify their status with the Federal Government, undefined nonrecognition is an incomprehensible non-policy. The tribes have not been able to escape the historical circumstances and living conditions all

---

[116] "Forgotten But Not Gone." *City on a Hill Press,* 19 May 2011, www.cityonahill press.com/2011/05/12/forgotten-but-not-gone/.

Indians share, but they have been unable to obtain the services which other tribes receive. They do not understand the reason for this discrepancy which defies logical explanation. The United States has permitted a flaw in the foundation of its Indian policy, in recognizing the beneficiaries of that policy a fact that itself is, incomprehensible to many people, Indians and non-Indians alike. Even if a clear institutional procedure for the recognition of tribes is adopted, there will be problems for the Indian communities to face. In every case, the Indian heritage of every group seeking recognition is undeniable, but it may well be difficult for several tribes to prove their identity and document their history. Educational opportunities were limited, and sometimes nonexistent in unrecognized Indian communities. Not only were these Indians unable to attend Federal Indian schools, but they were often excluded from both schools for blacks and schools for whites. When tribal leaders cannot write it is extremely difficult for them to present their case before the Federal Government. It may take a great deal of research to combat an offhand reply from a BIA official. Historical research is as difficult to finance as legal assistance is, so unless outside funding, or agencies aid these communities, their history remains buried. Commissioner Ada Deer addressed this point in the first Commission meeting: 'It is a tremendous burden on the tribe to take on the Department of the interior, take on the Congress ... there are a number of tribes that have been denied recognition, which may not catch the fancy of some foundation or other group."[117]

Less than one hundred years ago Missouri & Arkansas Ozark Indians could not disclose their race and cultures, tribe permitted, in public without facing eviction from their homes as they had no "legal" rights to the land. They as Indians in the Ozarks Plateau, in fear of hate, allowed their cultures to become invisible to the public. Only they knew their existence in the past,

---

[117] United States, Congress, "Final Report Submitted: to Congress May 17, 1977. Volume One of Two.", 1977, 478, 479.

they knew the whereabouts of their kin sprinkled throughout the hollers, caves, ridge lines, and valleys, they knew their land that their Grandfathers and Great-Grandfathers had given their all to tend to and the traditions that come with that heritage through their folk traditions, with the use of their folktales laying out for them the geographic area of the Ozarks.[118] Within the state it has almost become an accepted notion that all the Indians were removed from Missouri after 1845. Now after reading up to this point, and as the history provided has proven, I can state to you that I do not see how this understanding came to be as my family has roots in both the states of Arkansas and Missouri, and unless we are mistaken to our own history, which we are not, we are Indian.

---

[118] E. Joan Wilson Miller. "The Ozark Culture Region as Revealed by Traditional Materials." *Annals of the Association of American Geographers*, vol. 58, no. 1, 1968, pp. 51–77. JSTOR, www.jstor.org/stable/2561819.

CULTURAL IDENTITY:

Shine A Light on Me

For one to understand a way to put yourself in the shoes of a person living as an Inter Displaced Person in America I will reluctantly offer up my experience. As a child I was always told of both my cultures. I had experienced racism both for being a Coonass from Louisiana through my mother's lines, and for being an Irish Indian on my father's side, who's family came to California from Oklahoma in the past. I was never white enough to be considered white, yet I was not an Indigenous person. This was not because I am in lieu of Indian blood, heritage, and culture, but it is in fact because my family is from Native Americans who claimed Arkansas and Missouri as home, connected to the lands as peoples descendent from a mixed group of "Old Settlers and Southern Cherokee " from the Cherokee Nation, with roots to Nassayn peoples, Native American communities; Communities of which lived in states that refused to recognize Indians as anything more than savage beasts. I would like to quote Stephen Corrine when he stated, "All the years of calling the Indian a 'savage' has never made him one,"[119] and this fact reigns true in the Ozarks as well.

I have been told, by non-indigenous peoples and recognized Indians alike, that I do not have the right to be Indian because my Band is not federally recognized, but as we have gone over, this distinction of having rights to benefits through the BIA does not make you an Indian; so while this is a predominantly held thought, as promoted by federally recognized groups, there is no truth to it. Moving on, all my life I was raised as a

---

[119] Corry, Stephen. *Tribal Peoples for Tomorrows World.* (Freeman Press, 2012), 245.

multicultural person of Irish, Indian, and Cajun descent, and I never gave much thought into the responsibility that we all hold to properly represent our heritage until after my tour of duty, from 2010 to 2011, in Afghanistan where I worked with tribal communities. In Afghan culture the indigenous care about all aspects of their tribal life. There is an inherent responsibility for all who are born into the tribe to ensure the future generations know and understand their ways. The biggest revelation for me was their pride in what they were, whether they were Pashtun or Noori. Lack of formal education and illiteracy did not keep these people from continuing their folk traditions and culture in their communities. Everyone had a tribal identity and proudly spoke of it to anyone who was interested.

In stark contrast to the tribal peoples in Afghanistan, the Native communities in Missouri and Arkansas have not publicly celebrated their heritage until recently, thus becoming muted populations, as we have covered multiple times throughout this work. The communities were forced to hide away their heritage from the state governments. These enclaves had few educated peoples in the past, many individuals made moonshine in the hollers and lived sustaining lives off their fields due to racial discrimination and Jim Crow segregation. I can recall a story as told to me by my grandmother about my great-great grandfather Traymon Moore who was not allowed to enter certain places of business, and was refused service by others in Arkansas, his native state, because he was a Cherokee Indian. These Indigenous families in the Ozarks, like mine, did not write books about their histories as the settlers in the new world did; but they did keep their family ties within their own communities to protect themselves from removals, or death, as had happened before.

Often overlooked, or under considered when discussing the identities of Native Americans, is the alternative perspective. If I could, I would like to raise a series of questions to the reader. Starting with, "what if your heritage was judged and defined by an outside group of people, I.E., an outgroup, with no cultural ties to your peoples?" And now, "what if the only way you could prove your heritage was by making sure your culture fits into the stereotypical terms of what this outgroup my think it should be? Lastly, "how could anyone know your cultural heritage and history if they have not yet met you, and have not learned about the peoples that you claim your heritage from?" To answer these questions, I would like to present what I call the "Unrecognized Identity Predicament."

To understand what I call the Unrecognized Identity Predicament I would like to further present you with a thought experiment. I want you to consider that as far back as you can remember you were told that your ancestors were Native American, so to you your whole family is Native American, you were born Indigenous person and throughout your earlier school aged years you actively identified as an Indigenous person. Now imagine that one day the topic of race is presented in a discussion in one of the high school classes that you are taking, or your place of work, or at a social function, when you are then asked your racial identity. You go on to proudly proclaim that you are a Chickamauga Cherokee Indian, or Lumbee, or Saponi, or any other "unrecognized" faction. However, instead of moving on to the next person to share their heritage, or just letting the conversation naturally continue as it would, it is now sidetracked; For the first time someone is requiring you to prove your heritage through producing a government identification of some type showing you are from a "recognized" group.

Now let's say this plays out to where you find yourself being challenged by your class, or your Coworkers, possibly to include the heckling of your professor, or in the case of work you could be further asked about it by your bosses as some companies receive benefits for hiring federally "recognized" Native Americans, requesting that you show "proof" of your heritage in the form of a card from the government that states your amount of "Indian blood". This creates a problem because you are from an "unrecognized" group of peoples, you may also be from one of the many tribal bodies that holds a traditional practice of refusing to sign rolls or treaties, staying independent from the federal government, and thus unable to produce the documents requested. Now, in lieu of having this "official documentation" in your possession in the form of a "Certificate of Degree of Indian Blood," or abbreviated as "CDIB," your character is now left in question with those who may have some degree of influence over you, whether it be an employer, teacher, etc. It may lead to you getting accused of being dishonest as you are a fake Indian, having a negative impact on your promotability at your place of employment, or your credibility as a peer. Thus, among your associates you are viewed as a wannabe and mocked, leaving you to wonder just who you are, challenging your cultural identity, and at the same time discrediting you as a "truthful" person among your peers in the process because of preconceived notions that they may hold of what makes someone a Native American. For the first time, you wonder if not holding some card really makes you not an Indigenous person, and thus a fraud.

Now remember that in this thought experiment culturally and socially you have been defined as a Native American all your life. However, on paper you are "assimilated" because your family hails from a tribe that is not currently recognized. You grow up learning your indigenous ways, but now you are being told by people who do not know you or your culture that you are not what your family has always been, Native American. So, what does this mean about your family's ancestral practices? Does this mean they are not truly indigenous teachings as they were taught to you? Or does this mean that the teachings are real, but your ancestors were not Indigenous? The answer to these questions is no, your families would still be just as much historically Native American as any other family that is currently enrolled in one of the federally "recognized" Bands, Tribes, or Nations of any other Indians. However, regardless to the answer these "unrecognized" individuals are left with a sense of shattered self. What they once knew to be a truth is now a gray area in their life, manifesting itself as a social anxiety towards their own heritage and culture, or for others it might develop into a need for seclusion and isolation to steer clear of the outgroup that has challenged them.

Because American culture is heavily invested in the outcome of mass accomplishments of the whole group, such as the winning of wars, the construction of the Railways in the 1800s, the preservation of public lands in the early 1900s, and the creation of the public roadways under Eisenhower in the 1950s, Americans have a hard time understanding how lesser accomplishments, for example when a community establishes a church, or a spiritual grounds, can drive these smaller communities, such as those of Native Americans. Dr. Thomas examines how tribal institutions are different from that of those of modern American society in a lot of facets to include how they address tasks at hand. He states that, "Institutions, that is, those organizations a human community erects to do some tasks for itself, education of the young or whatever it might be, is in tribal societies simply an arrangement of relatives to do a particular task. And if one looks closely at those institutions, we will see that they follow the social form of their own tribal society, of that kin relationship. If a tribe is organized by clans, then one will see representation by clan in tribal councils, a governmental institution. In a military institution uncles might sponsor their nephews in war activity. Thus, all institutions in a tribe are relative arranging themselves together to accomplish some tasks. New institutions emerge. They are not planned. In modern urban life, when people perceive a task, they first plan- the most efficient organization to accomplish that task, fit themselves into the role slots of the newly created organization, then they take on the task. In tribal societies people first take on the task then the form of the organization emerges. After it continues for a few years, it will become sacredly sanctioned. If that institution lasts a generation, it will become traditional."[120]

Traditionalism is dictated by the generations that came before the current tribal body. Having their traditions judged by the outgroup does not mean that the indigenous factions in question

---

[120] Thomas, Robert K. *Mental Health: American Indian Tribal Societies.* works.bepress.com/robert_thomas/10/download/.

aren't valid, as the outgroups have no reference for what is considered "traditional" for the culture being discussed, and therefore have no base of understanding of the group, as often what is "traditional" is expected to also be historically based, but as stated by Dr. Thomas for Natives traditions can be established in short order, over the course of a generation. Some Native American groups, like those from the Southeastern states, as we have thoroughly gone over, traditionally hid from being listed on rolls. An example of a recognized group of Cherokees that had the same traditional practice of resisting assimilation was the Redbird Smith group, aka the Kee-too-wah Knight hawk society, which was a faction of Kee-too-wah in the late 1800s through the early 1900s who had separated from the Ross Faction led Cherokee Nation, the difference here being that, "most Nighthawks ... refused to comply", to sign the Dawes Rolls but, "the Dawes Commission enrolled Smith's defiant followers without their consent."[121] So they were later eligible to be federally recognized when the Cherokee Nation of Oklahoma was reestablished in the 1970s using the Dawes Rolls as the base Roll for their enrollment.

In short, any tribalized person is the reflection of their own tribal culture. The issue here is that you cannot judge an Indigenous community through the lens of standard American culture. This is because, "the first characteristic of North American Indian communities is that they are kin based. Now that does not come as a surprise to anyone, except to emphasize that the kin relationship was the only relationship in most North American Indian communities. The only person that a tribal Indian saw in his community until very recently was a kinsman. Everyone around you was a relative. The local unit, or community, of North American Indian groups varied in population size from about 100-300."[122] This is true for the Ozarks as well, as we have

---

[121] Weber, Micheal Lee. "Redbird Smith Movement." *The Encyclopedia of Oklahoma History and Culture*, www.okhistory.org/publications/enc/entry.php?entry=RE015.
[122] Thomas, Robert K. *Mental Health: American Indian Tribal Societies.* works.bepress.com/robert_thomas/10/download/.

covered, many factors kept the groups small, secluded, and reliant on their kin-based societies until modern times. Thus, what is traditional for the Native American societies are all variant, even if they have the same place of origin, such as they all came from the Cherokee Nation of Old. For example, the Chickamauga are a mix of Shawnee, Cherokee, and inter displaced Indigenous bands such as Nassayn peoples, that reformed, and re-organized, under Cherokee culture and religion. However, in modern day the Chickamauga factions in America follow similar, but different, traditional practices that are independent of each other, and that have developed based on the area and influences where they settled after leaving the lower Cherokee towns in the 1800s.

Another characteristic that falls outside of mass American culture of small American Indian communities is that they are, "extraordinarily responsive to the physical or natural environment", [123] which is vastly different than the big cities where the environment is second to the wants of man.[124] Bob Thomas states on this environmental impact that, "If one examines the customs of any particular tribal groups, one can see that their culture reflects a certain natural environment-- the houses, the marriage customs, whatever. If corn is introduced into a society where women have control over plants, they will no doubt take over gardening. The best marriage arrangement then is to leave them at their fields, and you go over there and live with them, if you are a man. That is what is called a matrilineal lineage in anthropology. And that social form reflects a certain 'environment.' What are called culture areas in North America, areas where tribes have customs in common, are tied to particular natural environments."[125] This tie to the land is not specific to Native Americans as it is also seen in rural Anglo farming communities in the

---

[123] Ibid.

[124] Smith, Gene. "Corporate Greed Is Killing the Environment." *Prime Political*, 5 Dec. 2018, primepolitical.com/2018/12/02/greed-killing-environment/.

[125] Ibid.

Appalachian mountains, in places like Clover Hollow where the residents have a similar connection to the lands their ancestors settled, and the continued conservation of them.[126] However, in the case of Clover Hollow the community is missing the other three elements that create a small nationality, which is uniquely apart of indigenous communities.

Both Social Identity and Cultural Identity theories come together to explain how connected a person's social group is to one's Identification of self. Cultural Identity theory can be used to explain how the group's influence can affect an individual's view of themselves. The "Collective trauma, be it through colonization (e.g., Aboriginal Peoples), slavery (e.g., African Americans), or war, has a dramatic impact on the psychological well-being of each and every individual member of the collective."[127] These experiences become a part of the cultural heritage which helps to define one's Cultural Identity. In Donald Taylor and Esther Usborne's article, *When I Know Who "We" Are, I Can Be "Me": The Primary Role of Cultural Identity Clarity for Psychological Well-Being*, published in the journal of Transcultural Psychology, the pair go over the importance of the need for clarity of cultural identity. They argue that having clarity in one's culture is fundamental for people to establish their personal identity, which is required to maintain a healthy psychological well-being overall.[128] They state in their article that the "Current understandings of those who have experienced collective trauma through colonization, slavery, intergroup conflict and terrorism, emphasize the impact that such horrific events have on the psychological well-being of every group member. Interventions for these individuals are often conceptualized and delivered at the

---

[126] Howell, Benita J. *Culture, Environment, and Conservation in the Appalachian South*. University of Illinois Press, 2002., 142.

[127] Taylor, Donald & Usborne, Esther. When I Know Who "We" Are, I Can Be "Me": The Primary Role of Cultural Identity Clarity for Psychological Well-Being. *Transcultural psychiatry*. 2010. 47. 93-111. 10.1177/1363461510364569.

[128] Ibid.

individual level through case-by-case efforts to rebuild psychological well-being." This study, in short, found that having a base understanding of one's own culture is directly linked to a person's self-esteem as the "theory of the self", argues that "the clarity of cultural identity is of central importance to the self-concept and to psychological well-being."[129]

This means that just as one's culture influences a person's overall mental health, so does one's Social Identity, and thus it cannot be discredited as an important part of the human experience. According to Tajfel and Turner's theory of social identity a main part of a person's "concept of self" is formed and influenced by their social groups to which they belong. Social Identity theory states that an individual does not just have one personal selfhood, but in fact multiple selves, and thus one holds various identities that they have formed in association with their affiliated groups influences. This means that a person might act differently in one social situation than they would in another dependent on the social groups they belong to. These situational influences can range from various groups such as, "their family, their country of nationality, and the neighborhood they live in, among many other possibilities,"[130] all coming together to align a person with multiple ingroups while at the same time creating their own personal sense of self. This sense of self that they have developed over the years than at any given time may, or may not, fit into what the person's original social grouping considered to be their values, as their sense of self is dependent to the influences that the other more dominating groups that they are a part of has over them, and to the situation at hand as well.

According to the theory of social identity a person's understanding of their own self-identity is fundamentally developed and influenced by the organizing groups they are from. Social

---

[129] Ibid.

[130] "Social Identity Theory (Tajfel, Turner)." *Learning Theories*, 4 Feb. 2017, www.learning-theories.com/social-identity-theory-tajfel-turner.html.

Identity Theory calls these different groupings that people are a part of "Social Categorizations." Examples of some of these social categories include one's racial groups, I.E. African American, Native American, or Asian, a person's profession such as if they are a blue-collar worker, student, or doctor, to a person's political affiliations. The theory states that if a person knows what categories they belong to than they can understand things about themselves better. It should be said once more that an individual can belong to several groups at the same time and thus can dictate their behavior accordingly to fit into one ingroup that might be in juxtaposition to another group that a person might be part of. An easy example of this would be a petty thief who still attends, and is a part of, a church community, as his professional life butts up against his spiritual one. So, then these groups are a base line for our "Social Identifications." This means that we tend to adopt the identity of the social groups that we belong to, and then we act in the same ways that other members of that group act, or in other words, we act in ways that make it easy for others from within the social group to identify us as one of their counterparts; this process is also known as trying to achieve homophily. After we categorize ourselves into groups that we identify with, we then tend to compare our ingroups against others. According to Social Identity Theory we then try to maintain our self-esteem by comparing our ingroups favorably against other outgroups.

This then leads to one of the most common problems for those faced with the "Unrecognized Identity Predicament," which is, becoming muted out of history moving forward in time. This is because if an ingroup is taught to sectionalize themselves from others of that group due to factional divisions then, at some point, they become a memory for the group they separated from. For instance, even though a person may be a part of an ingroup that identifies as Native American the perception of their group to other outgroups that also may share a similar history may not be accurate. Such is the case with "unrecognized tribal groups" in comparison to the other Indigenous outgroups, as each outgroup has different rates of what it means to be Indigenous, and thus there can be multiple meanings that can also contradict each other. Every group has their own identities and while they may share a broad term for Categorization purposes, such as Native American, the traumas faced by one's ancestors has an influence on how they live their lives, and this then leads to the group becoming muted over time, as they are not recognized as having their own distinct cultural experience to the outgroups and thus become ignored. Not only does this influence the group, but as we have just gone over, it has devastating effects on the individual as well.

BAD BLOOD IN MODERN INDIAN AFFAIRS:

Indian Gaming, Disenrollment, & the Issue of Federal Funds

In the 21st century the Issue of Federal Funds has created a monetary value to add on to the issues that face native Americans. In the past Native Americans have been divided by governments that wanted to oppress or assimilate them. Now Native American tribes are forced to compete against each other for a piece of an almost mythical pie of allocated federal funds that are meant to help to preserve Native America. There seems to be this Idea among native American tribes that if more tribes become federally recognized then the pie will get smaller. Because of the monetary gain that has become associated with being a federally recognized tribe there is an understanding that all tribes that seek Federal recognition must be fraudulent. However, this logic is fundamentally flawed because not all tribes were recognized by the United States of America at the same time or under a standard treaty, many tribes lost trust and would not sign new treaties with the government opting to stay in hiding rather than assimilate, while others were forced to assimilate as the federal government was disbanding tribes under the Indian termination policy from the mid-1940s to the mid-1960s.[131] So to say that a tribe that finally feels like they have some representation within a state to seek their status as a Native American tribe is a fraudulent one because they are not recognized already is to

---

[131] "Staying Indian in Ohio (2015)." *YouTube*, YouTube, 7 Jan. 2015, https://www.youtube.com/watch?v=hp15X7VMwak.

say that the influence of racism, social injustices, and oppression that the tribe has experienced throughout the course of their history wasn't real; whether there continues to be a threat that creates fear within a body of peoples, or whether the fears are imagined for a tribe based off their shared past experiences, the fact still stands that fear can cause people to live in an oppressed state well after the threat has been removed.

Native America has just recently been afforded opportunities for monetary ventures. It was not until the introduction of new legislation in the late 1980s and 1990s, such as the Indian Gaming Regulatory Act of 1988 or the Indian Arts and Crafts Act of 1990, that tribes have had the opportunity for monetary gain of any substance. It is common to find that among the tribes that currently seek Federal recognition most have been organized as their own tribal bodies in lieu of, or in loose connection to, governance from another tribe for decades, such as the before mentioned lumbee who have been trying for more than a century to be recognized by the federal government,[132] thus the idea that these tribes are fraudulent because they are in it for a monetary gain is ridiculous as most communities spend their own money and resources on the process of becoming recognized. In most cases the tribes enlist the help of volunteers who work on them on time on collecting the proper documents and ect needed for the Federal Acknowledgement Process. The volunteers are often the tribal members themselves and, in some cases, other non-tribally affiliated people, such as Linda Carr who worked with the Southern Cherokee in her retirement on their petition for the Federal Acknowledgement Process,[133] all come together

---

[132] By. "With a New Bill, North Carolina's Lumbee Tribe Continues to Push for Federal Recognition." *NativeBiz*, 17 Apr. 2015, https://nativebiz.wordpress.com/2015/04/17/with-a-new-bill-north-carolinas-lumbee-tribe-continues-to-push-for-federal-recognition/.

[133] Matthews, Darla Gene. "The Southern Cherokee Indian Tribe Tsalagi Tsuganwv (Also Known as the Treaty Tribe)." Missouri, United States, Newburg, 30 Apr. 2015, 5.

to fight for the right to legally be what they know they are, Native Americans. Even federally recognized tribes face issues with monetary value. One of the things that we see quite frequently now is that of disenrollment.

Disenrollment is the practice of "disenrolling" a member from a tribe, so they are no longer recognized as a Native American within that tribal body. Time and time again we have seen families pushed out of their own tribal bodies based on either bad blood between families, politics, or for their lack of blood after the blood-quantum requirement for the tribe has been risen. While it maybe hard to believe Disenrollment is an issue that is happening in Indian Country at an alarming rate. Gaming Tribes are partaking in the practice of kicking members out of their tribe claiming falsely that the families are not Native Americans or that they are not affiliated with the tribe. The government seems to turn a blind eye to the situation as "A few folks at BIA headquarters simply decided from behind closed doors that the agency should no longer get involved in disenrollment controversies. And the rest is modern history."[134] However, the BIA isn't the one to put the blame on here because they are tied by other laws that protect Indigenous rights such as Article 33 of the UN Declaration of the Rights of Indigenous People which states:

> Indigenous peoples have the right to determine their own identity or membership in accordance with their customs and traditions. This does not impair the right of indigenous individuals to obtain citizenship of the States in which they live.

> Indigenous peoples have the right to determine the structures and to select the membership of their institutions in accordance with their own procedures.

---

[134] Galanda, Gabriel S. "Disenrollment Is a Federal Action." *Indian Country Today,* Indian Country Today, 10 Mar. 2015, https://indiancountrytoday.com/archive/disenrollment-is-a-federal-action.

This means that the tribes themselves, as sovereign nations, sets their own criteria for a person to be considered a tribal member. This means that the State and federal governments have no real say when it comes to tribal membership; in the end it is still up to sovereign nations to decide who is enrolled. In these modern times in Native America, we now have a situation where corrupt tribal leadership can exploit their tribal sovereignty to legally justify the need for the disenrollment of its tribal members. The tribes can do this by voting in amendments to their tribal constitutions and by disputing the accuracy of the original tribal rolls that established the tribe. The problem we face in looking at disenrollment or any other problems regarding tribes is that the history of an oppressed group is full of inconsistencies between the official records and the oral history of tribes themselves.

In the past the oppressed seem to have had no legal defense and thus do not have an accurate history that was officially recorded by the United States. Whither it be Native Americans versus the United States Government as a whole, or the oppression of bands within the greater tribal body by the other groups that descend from the historical tribe, such as the oppression of unrecognized Cherokees at the hands of the federally recognized Cherokee Nation of Oklahoma, the fact still stands that family ties and racism were deeply embedded in 19th century politics that in turn shaped the history that people cite as truth today ignoring that some of the facts got skewed in the process. In terms of disenrollment these gaps in history allow for it to be rewritten to exclude people. Such is the case of the families who were disenrolled from The Pechanga Band of Luiseno Mission Indians to include the descendants of Pablo Apis the chief that signed the 1875 treaty between the tribe and the United States of America establishing their reservation in California.[135]

---

[135] "'This Is All Stolen Land': Native Americans Want More than California's Apology." *The Guardian*, Guardian News and Media, 21 June 2019, https://www.theguardian.com/us-news/2019/jun/20/california-native-americans-governor-apology-reparations.

Even if the history of a family is recorded it can easily be changed to write them out years after. Even if a family comes from a chief that created the formally recognized tribe or band, as seen with the Pechanga Band of Luiseno Mission Indians, they can still fall victim to being disenrolled. In the history of the United States of America there has been extreme oppression of Native Americans. The negative influences of past prejudices can be seen well into the 20th century. Not discussed in our history books is how racism thrived in reference to Native Americans well into the 1970s. The eugenics programs in America utilized by the courts at the turn of the century continued in secret with the ordering of forced sterilization of Native American women. On November 6, 1976, the Government Accounting Office (GAO) finished an investigation into forced sterilizations among native women finding that, "IHS performed 3,406 sterilizations between 1973 and 1976" which is equivalent to "sterilizing 452,000 non-Native American women." Forced sterilization through eugenics fell out of popular favor after WWII. However, it was practiced well into the 1980s with devastating results for the minority populations targeted by the laws. The justification for the practice was to end bad blood lines basing their concerns with heredity. With all the problems presented by the federal and state governments in the past, as well as the treatment of the unrecognized Native peoples in modern times, in terms of tribal politics, it is easy to see why tribes stayed secluded until recent times. For the Southern Cherokee, the drive towards federal recognition came when elders started to question how they would achieve the preservation of their heritage. Darla Gene Matthews writes in their petition for recognition that, "one evening 12 years ago, my husband, Steve Matthews, after discussion with several other Southern Cherokee citizens, including Johnnie Gray, George Humphrey, Charles Wilcock and a few others, said to me, 'I wouldn't know what to say to my grandchildren were they to come to me years from now and ask, 'why didn't you do something to protect my heritage?' He continued, 'we have to do something, not only for the current tribe for all those who come after us!' I agreed." From that point forward, other members of the tribe joined in the quest and passion has both fueled and driven the Southern Cherokee forward. [136] The seclusion was for self-preservation not monetary gain as proposed by people using terms like "fake Indians," "wannabes," and "fraudulent tribes." While there are fraudulent people and tribes that does not mean that everyone is furthermore it is a great injustice to attest such terms to groups of Indigenous peoples who have lived through and continue to face oppression, as result of their heritage, just because they splintered off from a greater historical tribe or tribal confederation in the past.

This notion that being a member of a "federally recognized group" means that you are a "real" Native American, or have certified blood through a governmental organization, is new in our society. Recently we did see a push for greater understanding of tribal populations from the Obama administration, but it was one sided with the focus only put on tribes that have federal recognition. This is because the federal government, through the current policies in place, recognizes federally acknowledged groups as the only "real" Indians they have to deal with through trust doctrine, ignoring the groups of who they view as "unrecognized" with devastating consequences. Just exactly how the Unrecognized peoples were ignored during the Obama years, while simultaneously other Native American groups were being praised, is explained by Valentin Lopez, a member of the Amah Mutsun tribe, stating, "They made a big show of it and that was beautiful, and yes, there were a hundred tribes there meeting at the White House but not one of them was a federally unrecognized tribe. ... And the unrecognized tribe has never been reached out to by the government."[137] The main problem

---

[136] Matthews, Darla Gene. "The Southern Cherokee Indian Tribe Tsalagi Tsuganwv (Also Known as the Treaty Tribe)." Missouri, United States, Newburg , 30 Apr. 2015, 6.
[137] "Forgotten But Not Gone." *City on a Hill Press,* 19 May 2011, www.cityonahillpress.com/2011/05/12/forgotten-but-not-gone/.

with defining a tribe, or an individual, as a "real Indian" because they are federally recognized is that it sets up an idea that one's "Indianness" is tied to the United States political system, which is not the case. It also is fundamentally flawed because it creates a situation in where some Indigenous groups are most certainly unable to meet the requirements due to the long-lasting effects of colonialism. Under the guidelines provided by the Federal Acknowledgment Process there is no consideration for the historical racism and indigenous erasure that has prevented groups from proving they are from a historical tribe of Native Americans. How can one prove in the current day, as required in the Federal Acknowledgement Process, their existence from a historical tribe if both the federal and state governments legally denied the Nations the right to do so without the fear of forcible removals, or death, in the past?

The question segues us into what I would consider one of the main issues facing the scholarly works being done on the Unrecognized indigenous peoples of the Americas today. Being the issue of the overall impact of colonialism on tribal societies, as well as the perspectives held by the different factions of tribal peoples on their own "self-identities," and what qualifies someone as Native American. What I mean by this is that some tribes have taken to blood quantities to define their "Indianness" with members referring to the others in their group based off the blood quantum that they hold. This is done in a different way than how the historical gas lighting is done using topics of degrees of blood, as we have covered when discussing actions taken by the Ross faction, and thus, later the Cherokee Nation of Oklahoma and the federal government in an attempt to change the narrative of Cherokee history; while it is still the political entities grouping each other as "full-bloods", or "half-bloods", to say just how much "Indian" a person is, however it is also accompanied by disenfranchisement once blood quantum has dropped below a certain criteria. While other tribes have taken different routes to define membership such as granting it through one's heritage to a person that was on their historically recorded rolls. This is to say that these tribes define the enrollment of people not dependent to their blood amounts, but rather, through their historical links to their tribal body.

Regardless to how a group defines their membership within their government, or in other words at an elite level, the folk culture of a tribe often still segregates between their own membership, in lieu of the elite definition, counting others within the group as more, or less, "Indian" depending on different social factors that may affect their community. For example, I have found it to not be uncommon, when at intertribal events such as a Powwow or Homecoming, to find lines drawn within tribes between the tribal members based on their current locations of inhabitants. This creates a situation where there are opposing groups, such as the city, or "urban Indians," and those that stayed on the Reservation, or "Rez Indians," equating a person's current home of residence as a defining factor to the persons "Indianness." With the acculturation of Native Americans into urban areas, even among federally recognized groups people have taken to using dog whistle terms, such as "registered voter," to claim that they hold more "Indianness" than others through their ability to influence the Reservation, looking to things such as their voting rights to establish who holds more value as an Indian as some tribes only allow those who live on the Reservation to vote on tribal affairs.

The most common reason that I have seen for the distinction between tribal members is that it is done in an attempt to frame those that are not from the Reservation as, "less Indian," because of the perceived notion that they have left the area for unjustified reasons, from leaving to become "white," or thinking they are "to good for the Rez," or to believing that "they don't follow tribal traditions because they live in the city," disregarding the multitude of valid reasons for why people leave. Often, it is not recognized that Indigenous cultures still survive within the urban context once they have been removed from their homelands, as seen with "The Reservation" neighborhood in Baltimore.[138]

Each indigenous faction, due to the various amounts of European influences placed on them at various times throughout their histories, all hold their own metrics on what they use to define their "Indianness," thus making Indianness as a concept relative as the metrics used to define it are varying between, and specific to, each indigenous group. As a result, what is used by a group to determine what make someone Indian is not easily identified as what is considered important to a tribe, in terms of their "Indianness" that is, as it is shaped by political, regional, and social influences placed on them, as what matters to one tribal body might not matter to another indigenous group. An easy example of this, "Relativity of Indianness," that we have already covered is blood quantum. Phyllis Stanton speaks to this issue of colonial influences on the indigenous populations, and their resulting varying perceptions of "Indianness," when she talks on Bob Thomas's views on indigenous erasure, in where she writes, "embroiled in a seemingly endless cycle of 'powerless politics,' these societies, especially those living on reservations, have long struggled against the preemptive elements of colonial processes that have systematically overwhelmed almost every major indigenous institution. In recent struggles to maintain and/or regain control of land, education, economies, religions, and identities, native peoples have had to overcome what Thomas called 'deprivations of existence' that left in some cases, multi-generational gaps in the reserves of collective cultural, historical, political, and scientific memory. As he often asserted one of the main depravations of experience due to colonialism is the understanding

---

[138] Ict. "A Quest to Reconstruct Baltimore's American Indian 'Reservation'." *IndianCountryToday.com,* Indian Country Today, 24 Apr. 2019, newsmaven.io/ indiancountrytoday/opinion/a-quest-to-reconstruct-baltimore-s-american-indian-reservation-mzTrtnNO-UmjJ2zmb1Ok2g/.

of how we (Native Americans) got where we are today. ”[139] The term, coined by Gayatri Spivak, that is used to describe the colonizer's effective erasure of the histories of an indigenous peoples is "epistemic violence", or in other words the lost or destroyed "documentation of indigenous voices that would have provided a more complete understanding of the impact and influence of colonial contact on the original peoples".[140] In essence, epistemic violence has created gaps in many aspects of culture and history for Native American peoples around the Americas, but that doesn't make them any less valid as indigenous communities.

Since their first contact with Christian nations, within their perspective lands, Native Americans have experienced epistemic violence because of western ethnocentrism to varying degrees within the United States of America. I feel that the epistemic violence on the Native American folk societies because of the folk–urban continuum goes highly understated, especially in places like the Ozarks. The folk-urban continuum was first presented by Robert Redfield in his study, The Folk Culture of Yucatan, in where he tries to illustrate the dichotomy between the folk societies and the urban ones that they encounter. He theorizes that the folk life of the Yucatan lost its community's isolation through their contact with the urban setting, thus they became more heterogenous, with their adoption of western economic practices in their marketplace, concluding that increased contact with any dissimilar society results in change resulting in the death of the original folk culture.[141]

However, the American Anthropologist Sol Tax rebutted Redfield's writings on the folk culture of the Yucatan making

---

[139] Pavlik, Steve, and Robert K. Thomas. *A Good Cherokee, a Good Anthropologist: Papers in Honor of Robert K. Thomas.* (American Indian Studies Center, 1998), 291.

[140] Ibid., 291.

[141] "Here Is Your Essay on Folk Urban Continuum." *PreserveArticles.com: Preserving Your Articles for Eternity,* 15 Oct. 2011, www.preservearticles.com/social-science/here-is-your-essay-on-folk-urban-continuum/13508.

the case that an outside society's world view can bring changes and dependent characteristics of a folk society without having any change in its independent characteristics.[142] Meaning that the influences of the urban setting can change the folk society in some ways without overtly materializing within their culture. This "cultural crossover" influences the perceived stoppage of the development of the Indigenous societies to the outside communities. For example, what is often not considered for Native Americans is that those who have moved into urban settings, or vice versa, those who have had an urban setting thrust upon them, often still hold onto, and pass down the teachings of their own folk societies to their future generations, and thus the urban societies, have an influence on the original folk culture that was first in place, but that by no way means that the folk culture then ceases to exist. Just as I have stated before, I would like to argue that there is more "cultural crossover" between societies in what Redfield defines as the folk-urban continuum, and that this cultural crossover was more problematic than it has past been thought, as it has gone on to help ensure that the only official Indians are those currently that hold a dialogue with the federal government leaving the Unrecognized indigenous populations as muted groups unable to communicate their positions to the powers that be in the United States.

So, then this begs us to ask just what exactly is a muted group? As explained in the muted group theory within the discipline of Communications, as it was created by Edwin Ardener and Shirley Ardener in 1975, a muted group is a marginalized set of peoples that are excluded, and thus muted, using language. So, in terms of the unrecognized tribes the language that is used to marginalize, and thus exclude them, is that of Legal English; since the 1970s this has been compounded by the historical gas lighting, cultural erasure, and the gatekeeping done by federally recognized groups against unrecognized factions. Before the creation

---

[142] Ibid.

of the Federal Acknowledgment Process, or FAP for short, the unrecognized tribes in America had members who were represented within the federal government as they served on task forces to address issues that were then facing Native Americans in the United States.[143] However, since the creation of the FAP the courts have been used to exclude unrecognized peoples through complicated legalese. The courts have somehow developed the view that Unrecognized tribes have majestically underwent an assimilation process in where they lost their Indigenous folk cultures because of having been exposed to Anglo societies. Simply put the use of Legal English as a, "Language serves its creators better than those in other groups who have to learn to use the language as best they can", and without adequate access to legal resources these unrecognized people have lost almost all their footing within the political spectrum as they cannot properly explain their plights.[144] After these issues caused by colonialism, such as becoming muted groups and the effects of indigenous erasure on their cultures & histories, unrecognized peoples now have to deal with the fact that recognized tribes, as the dominant indigenous cultures represented within the federal discussion of recognition, also set out to keep other unrecognized groups muted as they now feel that they hold the only right to represent their shared ancestors and histories; to the point where some recognized tribes have spent millions on funding research and lobbying the government to keep unrecognized tribes viewed as "fakes", "pretendians", and "wannabes".

According to the Cherokee Nation their official stance is that "everyone with Cherokee ties left Arkansas after 1828."[145] Even though, as we have covered this is not the case, as explained

---

[143] United States, Congress, "Final Report Submitted: to Congress May 17, 1977. Volume One of Two.", 1977, 1–591.

[144] West, Richard, and Lynn H. Turner. *Introducing Communication Theory Analysis and Application*. McGraw-Hill Education, 2018.

[145] "A Hidden History: Dwight Mission." *The Boiled Down Juice*, 20 May 2014, www.boileddownjuice.website/a-hidden-history-dwight-mission/.

by Stewart-Abernathy from the Arkansas Archeological Survey, "there were at least a few Cherokee families [who] originally left for Oklahoma only to slip back into Arkansas years later to escape the Cherokee civil war. There are even reports that some Cherokee families returned to the area generations later... seeking to escape the intense poverty and desperation of life on the Oklahoma reservation."[146] So clearly the Cherokee had a connection to the lands in Arkansas well after 1828 with a strong presence in the Arkansas River Valley where it is pretty well-known that, "Everywhere you turn in the river valley area you'll find people in both white and black communities who claim Cherokee ancestry."[147] More recently some scholars have used terms like "racial shifters" to describe these groups stating that their heritage is nothing more than a result of a search for a meaningful life equating their families experiences into nothing but false claims as a way to repudiate their whiteness. In the words of anthropologist Circe Sturm all they are doing is trying to find a "remedy for the 'ills of the modern, neoliberal age' while keeping their white privilege."[148] However it is completely erroneous to apply this term to every undocumented or unrecognized Native American group. While I do agree that there are racial shifters, or the Asa Carters, Ward Churchills, and Rachel Dolezals of the world if you will, who do claim a minority identity with no validity to their statements, this does not mean that every unrecognized person or group falls into this category.

The problem is in how modern-day American's racially identify. Many U.S. Citizens "Self-identify"[149] as Native Americans.

---

[146] Ibid.

[147] Ibid.

[148] Steineker, Rowan Faye. *"Becoming Indian: The Struggle over Cherokee Identity in the Twenty-First Century by Circe Sturm (review)."* The American Indian Quarterly, vol. 38 no. 3, 2014, 400-402. Project MUSE,

[149] Cushman, Ellen. "Toward a Rhetoric of Self-Representation: Identity Politics in Indian Country and Rhetoric and Composition." *College Composition and Communication*, vol. 60, no. 2, 2008, pp. 321–365. JSTOR, www.jstor.org/stable/20457062.

These people do nothing more than check a box on a census or official form to obtain heritage; they never provide any real proof to claims of their ancestry. Most of the time these people are the common everyday Americans who self-identify as an American Indian because they have heard stories of one of their great-great-great grandmothers who was either a Native American princess, an Indian slave, or were a kidnapped and/or a lone indigenous child that was rescued by a white savior, as explanations for why the rest of their families were not Native Americans. Versus the individual who has a "Self-Representation" as a Native American.[150] These people have a "self-representation" as Indians who have an identity claim that is supported by evidence. The evidence they use to support their claim are their historical family ties to their communities and their migrations as groups across the lands, proven links of families through genealogical and historical documents, and their shared community identity that has developed within their group over the course of generations.

Today there is a dangerously high amount of Native American groups that are just people who "self-identify" as Native Americans coming together, with no proven claims to their heritage, while at the same time demanding rights reserved for Native Americans. However, just because these groups exist does not mean that other groups of unrecognized Indians, who have lived as indigenous enclaves with a long held self-representation as Native Americans, do not exist as well. Such is the case with my family. For example, I was raised as an Indian, as we have covered, beyond just checking a box, just as my father was, and just as his parents were in Oklahoma and Arkansas before him. But I am multi-cultural as my mother is Cajun; I still have a "Self-Representation" as a Native American that has been a part of my life since youth, as I am a descendant of the Nichols & Bunch families of Saponi Indians in Grayson County Virginia,

---

[150] Ibid.

and as a descendant of Chickamauga Treaty Party Cherokees from both my Smiths & Fletcher families in the Boston Mountains of Arkansas. I claim from my Grokett family in Oklahoma both Chickasaw and Choctaw bloodlines. My Grokett family moved into Indian Territory in the early 1800s as some of the first Indian settlers to the area of Indian City, the lands of what would later become Anadarko, Oklahoma. Our ancestors passed our information through oral traditions, bible records, etc., of our elders, our families, and our tribes. But we must also consider that even if our peoples each respectively kept their own written account of ourselves that was historically preserved, it would still not matter in this case do to epistemic violence, as we are captive to the guidelines of historical methods of research, as well as the social interpretation of Ozark history and how it is applied to the study of Indians in the area, and their removal thereafter due to Missouri's creation as a slave state.

We must understand that the study of history regarding many Indian nations is applied in the same fashion as one would recount actions in a war. The United States of America tends to look at the Indian nations history as starting where the disturbance was introduced between the Tribal Nation and the United States, and thus the Native Nation's history is written and interpreted from there on, fading away in the history books after the conflict is resolved for the United States. However, we as Native Americans, know our history starts long before and well after the existence of the United States as we share family bonds that last beyond the words stated between nations when they meet pen to paper while signing treaties. We are diverse. We are tribes that consist of families who share a common experience, we are enclaves of mixed ethnicities, but we are united by our blood and culture. I truly do not believe that someone can be a fraction of their heritage.

Speaking of fractions, let us segue into a further examination of the issue of blood quantum, as it is as inaccurate today for determining someone's Indianness as it was in the past, as Indian tribes are not defined by blood alone but by their shared culture, genealogical connection, and historical land links to their communities. Historically, racist views shaped the outcome of the Dawes Rolls, in where one can find that siblings of the same parents were recorded as having varying degrees of Native American blood based off their skin tones. Some tribal citizens who were enrolled as Freedmen, which were both of African and Indian heritage, were denied their Indian identity being only counted as Freedmen in the final rolls with no recorded Indian blood; and then constantly denied recognition until very recently as we have covered. The idea of blood quantum was created to determine at which point an individual stops being Indian and thus becomes an assimilated American citizen. The goal was the genocide of the American Indian through assimilation by applying a cut off number of 25% of Indian blood as the definition to who was Indian in the past. The U.S. government wanted to kill the cultures and dilute the blood lines until tribes no longer existed. This practice came to fruition in the form of the Indian termination policy starting in the mid-1940s and ending in the mid-1960s.[151] The federal government has since dropped the 25% blood quantum requirement leaving enrollment issues up to the tribal bodies themselves.

The Cherokee Nation in Oklahoma does not have a minimum blood quantum, their requirement for membership is that one must descend from enrollees of their tribal roll, being that of The Dawes Rolls. However, The Dawes Rolls were fundamentally wrong for all the tribes recorded by the commission, and the Cherokee Nation has no problem pointing to this when politically lucrative for them as we have seen. The "Dawes Commission chairman Tams Bixby estimated that only one in ten claimants placed on the Chickasaw and Choctaw rolls by the courts were entitled to citizenship. In the end thousands of fraudulent claims were granted over the objections of the leaders of the Five

------

[151] "The Termination Era." *Native American Netroots*, nativeamericannetroots. net/diary/1511.

Tribes— thousands of people became new tribal citizens."[152] The Dawes rolls were created by Henry Dawes who believed, "selfishness was the root of civilization" philosophizing that, "The separate farm is the door to civilization"[153] the logic being that if Indians agreed and signed to the terms of the Dawes rolls it would help to speed up assimilation as, "To get on the Dawes Rolls, Native Americans had to 'anglicize' their names. Rolling Thunder thus became Ron Thomas and so forth. This bit of 'melting pot' chicanery allowed agents of the government, sent to the frontier to administer the Act, to slip the names of their relatives and friends onto the Dawes Rolls and thus reap millions of acres of land for their friends and cronies." Senator Henry M Tiller even stated, "the real aim of [The Dawes Act] is to get the Indians' land and open it up for settlement".[154] The result, not for seen by the Ross faction, of the number of fraudulent enrollments was that "These dubious enrollees, with rights secured, often then led the charge to destroy the tribal governments and Indian way of life…. the Cherokees ended up running out of land for real Cherokee people…. The final rolls, completed in 1906, divided the 'Five Civilized Tribes' into citizens along racial lines— each enrollee was listed as a citizen by Indian 'blood,' freedman, or intermarried white. Where once notions of citizenship rested on family and community, citizenship now was a matter of formal governmental rolls."[155]

The Cherokees who did not sign, or were rejected from, the Dawes Rolls were denied tribal citizenship within the Cherokee Nation and forced to live as undocumented individuals with

---

[152] Miller, Mark Edwin. *Claiming Tribal Identity: the Five Tribes and the Politics of Federal Acknowledgment.* University of Oklahoma Press, 2013, 93.

[153] Hagan, William T. "Private Property, the Indian's Door to Civilization." *Ethnohistory*, vol. 3, no. 2, 1956, 126. JSTOR, www.jstor.org/stable/480525.

[154] "Dawes." *First Nations Issues of Consequence,* www.dickshovel.com/cleansing.html.

[155] Miller, Mark Edwin. *Claiming Tribal Identity: the Five Tribes and the Politics of Federal Acknowledgment.* University of Oklahoma Press, 2013, 96.

no rights in any governmental body recognized by the United States, in a state the United Nation calls Inter Displaced Peoples, until 1924, with the passage of the Indian Citizenship Act. Now the Cherokee Nation states on their website that, "If your ancestor did not live in this area during that specific time period, they will not be listed on the Dawes Rolls."[156] Negating the fact that historically white men decided who were tribal members when the "former U.S. senator Henry L. Dawes, retired architect of the earlier allotment legislation, was charged with determining who qualified for membership. With this maneuver the federal government usurped the Five Tribes' fundamental right to determine their citizenship requirements."[157] The Cherokee Nation under cuts the history of Indian Territory by downplaying the multiple diasporas of Cherokees that had happened throughout the 1800s, until well after the Civil War, the power plays made by the individual factions, and the U.S. government itself selecting to focus on a narrative in where they are the victim in every situation, and as a result there were many families who held less than uncertain social and legal standings within the Cherokee Nation for decades.

For the Old Settlers and Southern Cherokee within the bounds of Indian country these families lived primarily within the CooWeeScooWee & Canadian Districts of the Cherokee Nation, and in small towns like Coffeyville that could be found along the Cherokee- Kansas border, and in Missouri, Arkansas, and Texas.[158] After the Civil War, with the post-war politics of Indian

---

[156] "About Citizenship." *Cherokee Nation*, cherokee.org/Services/Tribal-Citizenship/Citizenship.

[157] Miller, Mark Edwin. *Claiming Tribal Identity: the Five Tribes and the Politics of Federal Acknowledgment.* University of Oklahoma Press, 2013, 90.

[158] S. D. Barclay to Principal Chief, July 19, 1878, Folder 10, Box O-21, Oochalata (Charles Thompson) Collection, WHC; American Sunday-School Union, The Fiftieth Annual Report of the American Sunday-School Union, 1874 (Philadelphia: American Sunday-School Union, 1874), 93; Painter, Exodusters, 113 – 115; Bryan M. Jack, Saint Louis African American Community and the Exodusters (Columbia: University of Missouri Press, 2007), 95.

Territory, the loss of Cherokee lands in the treaty of 1867, migration of family groups and their re-settlement in new locations in Missouri, Arkansas, Texas, and Kansas, intermarriages and cultural exchange, all helped to complicate what was the "traditional" parameters for what it meant to be Cherokee.[159] These people were rejected from the tribe and lived in family groups and bands, or in some cases they assimilated into the broader American communities that they lived in, as a result. Either way they were being forced into American culture and further away from being recognized as traditional peoples regardless to their personal practices.

Assimilation happened on the reservations as well as off them. At the turn of the 20th century, "the court language reveals the federal inclination to terminate tribes and assimilate Indians into the mainstream."[160] The U.S. government then set up schools to help aid in this endeavor shipping Indigenous children far away from their families. An example of these schools was the Carlisle Indian Industrial School, which was, "the first off-reservation boarding school and began the social experiment of assimilation of Native Americans into American culture." They did this with little regards for the children themselves as, "for almost 40 years, from 1879 to 1918, the school sought to civilize 'savage' Indian children. Richard H. Pratt, founder of the Carlisle Indian Industrial School, believed that the school was the solution to the 'Indian Problem.' To successfully carry out the mission to assimilate and rehabilitate, Pratt believed that the school must, 'Kill the Indian, save the man."[161] The boarding school experience is not unique to just one area or tribe. When cultures meet, they adapt and blend or, in the case of American

---

[159] SMITHERS, GREGORY D. *CHEROKEE DIASPORA: an Indigenous History of Migration, Resettlement, and Identity.* YALE UNIVERSITY PRESS, 2018., 185.
[160] Miller, Mark Edwin. *Claiming Tribal Identity: the Five Tribes and the Politics of Federal Acknowledgment.* University of Oklahoma Press, 2013., 100.
[161] Satterlee, Anita. "The Carlisle Indian Industrial School." *Eric Institute of Education Sciences* , 28 Oct. 2002, files.eric.ed.gov/fulltext/ED472262.pdf.

Indian history, one culture tries to destroy and eliminate the other. Bringing me to my next and final point.

Chief Bill John Baker is of mixed ethnicity, like many Cherokee citizens enrolled with the Cherokee Nation, he possesses 1/32nd degree of Cherokee blood, to put it into perspective this would be the same amount of blood quantum as claimed by Elizabeth Warren although she has no bases in her claims from what I can find, and he was the leader of the Cherokee Nation.[162] So my question is then this, how can a Nation claim that they are the only ones with true heritage when their base roll is known to have been corrupted to benefit the white agents whose aims were at killing Indian sovereignty through assimilation; going further, who then thinks it's just to give that nation the right to dictate the sovereignty of others or the sole claim to the heritage of the historic tribe just because they are recognized by the United States government now as having more authority to do so without any real reason as to why that is? We can also ask, speaking in outdated racial terms, how does having a white card issued by the United States of America to certify your 1/32nd Degree of Indian Blood, which is 3% Cherokee by Blood, make you more of a "red man" than an undocumented family of "full bloods" who in lieu of paperwork is labeled as "white", which all federally government groups know happened? The answer is it does not. "Recognized" or not they all share the same historical roots; they are all Cherokee. When we, as nations, bands, and tribal family groups, let our heritage be dictated and influenced by others, whether we share a common link in history as a tribe or not, we are allowing abuses of colonialism to continue against us. The action of allowing others to add their opinions or input about our history and place in the world, as the Bureau of Indian Affairs does when they go about the process of recognizing

---

[162] Althouse, Ann. "'For the Cherokee Nation, Warren Is 'Indian Enough;' She Has the Same Blood Quantum as Cherokee Nation Chief Bill John Baker."." *Althouse*, althouse.blogspot.com/2012/05/for-cherokee-nation-warren-is-indian.html.

new tribal bodies, is to let the oppression of our ancestors continue. When tribes start to comment saying that a tribe, or splinter
group, is "fake" because they left the main body of peoples in the
past then we, as curators of our history, are letting those tribes
say that the shared experiences and stories of what the petitioning party went through in the past was not real.

Often the argument against Missouri and Arkansas Indians
is that somehow, we gave up our identities, in the current day,
as Native Americans because our ancestors chose not to continue
with the groups of Cherokee in Oklahoma or in North Carolina that later became federally recognized. However, assimilation
was forced on all tribes resulting in 65% of Native peoples residing in urban areas today who have, at least in terms of mass society, assimilated to the dominant American culture.[163] Yet these
descendants from federally recognized tribes are still considered
"real Indians". Assimilation to Anglo society was a point used
to exclude groups at the turn of the century, yet it seems to be
ignored for the members of federally recognized Urban Indians
that exist in many major cities today. So, if assimilation is not
seen as wrong but as a part of a progressive Indian Nation then
why is it that it is still used to exclude groups of peoples from
their ranks?

Some tribal members from Federally Recognized Cherokee
tribes make it their mission to attack the possibility of any other
Cherokee Factions still being in existence today, other than the
three federally recognized tribes, making statements to support
their views like, "We have family stories and documents from
Cherokee Nation listing arrival and where they lived throughout the 1800's... In all of the stories that I have read by these old
ones in our archives have I ever found a story of Missing Cherokees that stayed in Missouri or Arkansas" going further they

---

[163] NAICCO. "'STAYING INDIAN IN OHIO.'" *YouTube*, YouTube, 7 Jan.
2015, www.youtube.com/watch?v=hp15X7VMwak.

claim, "the idea that LARGE groups of Cherokees hid out to account for the Really larger number of folks that still claim Heritage today is a bit much to believe", because according to them they have records of, "some 130,000 applicants and of that some 30,000 that they found were actually Cherokees from as far away as Hawaii and even POLAND that stayed in touch with the tribe" leading one to believe that since they had such a far reaching field of applicants than there is no way the smaller groups in the Ozarks wouldn't have been counted; this is small minded as we have already covered that there was ample fraud in their documents and the more likely scenario is that those numerous white families had people back in the old country as applicants. Political factions that splinter do not take full accountability for each faction. Understanding this to be a flaw in their logic they try to fight the idea of splinter groups by saying, "groups have splintered off and gone their own way throughout history, BUT they have kept in contact with the main body and were mentioned in Historical documents. Just like a group of Eastern Cherokees that moved near Stilwell in the 1870's or those that had come over the trail of tears to go back to North Carolina in the 1850's." Continuing to state, "We tended to cluster together in communities sharing a bond of Language and Culture."[164] This is however a blatant blanket statement that rewrites the history to make it seem as if Cherokees were all one group of peoples or united under one government as a tribe in the 1800s. When, as we have been over, just is not true is we were united under factions grouped by towns. But I will address these claims.

First, there is historical proof that groups did in fact leave out of Indian Territory as refugees heading back into the states of Arkansas and Missouri. Some of those that went back to Missouri and Arkansas went after the Treaty of 1846 was signed.

---

[164] "Missouri/Arkansas Cherokee." *PowWows.com - Native American Pow Wows,* 21 Jan. 2019, www.powwows.com/missouriarkansas-cherokee/.

this group was noted to have produced "360 refugees in Missouri"[165] with countless others living in hiding in both states; some of the groups have been noted to have been helped by General Matthew Arbuckle at Fort Gibson.[166] These Indian refugees faced violence from other Cherokee groups in Indian Territory, so they left the area settling lands as they felt fit. After the Civil War there is records of both "Cherokee boys and girls" attending schools in Arkansas. This was, "before the Cherokees had been able to reopen and carry on their own schooling."[167] There is no doubt that relationships formed during these times established the links for why Cherokee families would relocate to Arkansas. From this information we can also track how a big group can form from these small groups of Inter Displaced Peoples, or from other isolated groups during the 1830s-1960s in the Ozarks. To do this we can use the group of 360 peoples who left out of Indian Territory for Missouri as noted earlier for our example.

So, lets answer the question to just how many of this group could still possibly be around today? To low ball this answer for a total, we will say that only half of this refugee group reproduces each generation. In the United States of America in the 1850s the average household or family size was 6.7 members; this number was consistent from the 1600s to until about 1910.[168] Now using these figures it is time for us to do some basic math to show how a group can grow in isolation. Let us assume the household makeups for this group of 360 refugees consisted of the grandparents, the parents, one being the current head of house, and two or three children. If we only have half the group reproducing with only other members of this group, then that would still allow for at least 90 couples to produce children in the future.

---

[165] Dale, Edward E. "Arkansas and the Cherokees." *The Arkansas Historical Quarterly*, vol. 8, no. 2, 1949, 102. JSTOR, www.jstor.org/stable/40030604.
[166] Ibid., 103.
[167] Ibid., 111.
[168] Schoellman, Todd, and Mich`ele Tertilt. *Families as Roommates: Changes in U.S. Household Size from 1850 to 2000**. Aug. 2007.

If we then assume that a generation for this group is anywhere from 20-30 years long, then we can conclude that there has been somewhere between 5 to 8 generations that would have come from this group of Cherokee in Missouri since 1846. This group then would have been adding at least 180-270 people into their community after every generation. Today this family group of 360 Missouri Cherokee theoretically could have created at least nine hundred more people with the ability to have produced well over 2,100. So could a group, like the Southern Cherokee Indian Tribe, as Inter Displaced Peoples, after needing to find refuge after the final nail in the coffin struck them from their position as a respected faction in the Cherokee Nation came when they stayed in service to the Southern cause as apart of the 1st Cherokee Mounted Rifles, exist within the Missouri Ozarks with just over 500 enrolled members still living in their ancestral area and practicing their traditional ways today? Well, it looks like the historical record,[169] and the math seems to show that not only could they exist, but they could have also produced a population of considerable numbers much greater than they claim, in the timeline given. It should be stated as well that this is just quick math examining one possible group, excluding external factors like marrying outside of the group, adoptions, murder, disease, land encroachment, and polygamy practices with Cherokee couples frequently having children out of wedlock or possessing multiple wives,[170] which all could have affected a group's size in the long run in both positive and negative ways. The reality is that the numbers show that these Cherokees could have created big populations within some groups, all while at the same time having enclaves that produced quite lower numbers as well, due to the countless variables that can affect the math in the end.

---

[169] Dale, Edward E. "Arkansas and the Cherokees." *The Arkansas Historical Quarterly*, vol. 8, no. 2, 1949, 108. JSTOR, www.jstor.org/stable/40030604.

[170] Pavlik, Steve, and Robert K. Thomas. *A Good Cherokee, a Good Anthropologist: Papers in Honor of Robert K. Thomas.* (American Indian Studies Center, 1998), 59.

Looking to another isolated group that was better tracked we can see that the Eastern Band of Cherokee Indians had a population growing in a relative state of isolation as those that could be found in the Ozarks at the same time. Within this isolated existence the group grew from 2,540 to nearly 4,494 over the course of 36 years, or two generations as discussed, adding 1,954 people to their numbers from 1924 to 1960.[171] We see the end result is still the same, the population grows and thrives, just as these other smaller enclaves did, becoming bigger over the course of a few generations, even without any outside influence to the group, much like what has transpired in the Ozarks. However, because this group is "Recognized" their numbers are not disputed.

The Cherokee have never been just one group of people, or one language, but a widespread confederation of peoples as the Cherokee Nation of Old was in fact a federation built out of villages that historically worked independent from each other and were loosely aligned through culture and various political factions. Since the first records scholars understood that the lands in the historical Cherokee territory of the Southeast were so vast that they were put into four major groups by the new Anglo settlers. These settlers ended up grouping the peoples in 1751, into what we would now consider the first iteration of the Nation of Old, as reformed to deal with these various Anglo cultures. The area was split up into 13 hunting and trading districts which were closer to the ancient tribal groupings with an implied 14th district: "Nuntiale and a village or two" with other major towns like Hiwassee not being included in the groupings.[172] Clearly our cultures varied from the influence of other relations to the lands and other tribal groups causing such divisions among the federation, and as

---

[171] KUPFERER, HARRIET J. "THE ISOLATED EASTERN CHEROKEE." *Midcontinent American Studies Journal*, vol. 6, no. 2, 1965, 124–134. JSTOR, www.jstor.org/stable/40640560.
[172] "Cherokee Dialects & Divisions." *Cherokee Dialects*, www.rootsweb.ancestry.com/~tnpolk2/cherokeedialects.htm.

with any nation over time, sections of the community found new homes in places that better fit the needs of their peoples.

The choice made by groups to remove from the greater tribes should not be viewed as a bad, or even a misguided, one. Let's remember that the reason for the Dawes Act was to assimilate Native Americans in a misguided attempt to help to bring them into white culture through private land ownership.[173] While the leaders of the Cherokee Nation of Old did not believe in "owning" land the peoples were being told by the same government that had moved their grandparents from their homes back east, to assimilate to a society where private land ownership was pivotal to its existence. So why is it more believable that all the Tribal Bands, Family Groups, and Peoples stayed with the bigger Cherokee Nation, over the course of space and time, just because they shared culture, even though a federalized form of government was, and had in the past, went against fundamental Cherokee believes,[174] than it is to believe that the culture did sustain in smaller forms in the new lands that these tribal bands, family groups, and peoples inhabit today in areas like that of the Blue Ridge, Ozarks, and Appalachian Mountain ranges?

Now, I find it funny how these federally recognized people are quick to point out that the groups of refugees could not have formed bands after removing from their greater tribes in their new lands of inhabitants, when multiple groups have done just that in the past. I also am perplexed by the fact that the topic of the $5 Indian[175] is never really discussed when talking about

---

[173] "Cleveland Signs the Dawes Severalty Act." *History.com*, A&E Television Networks, 16 Nov. 2009, www.history.com/this-day-in-history/cleveland-signs-the-dawes-severalty-act.

[174] Arnold, Mary. "Land Tenure and Use in Native American Culture.", matriarchy.info/index.php?option=com_content&task=view&id=146.

[175] Landry, Alysa. "Paying to Play Indian: The Dawes Rolls and the Legacy of $5 Indians." *IndianCountryToday.com*, Indian Country Today, 21 Mar. 2017, newsmaven.io/indiancountrytoday/archive/paying-to-play-indian-the-dawes-rolls-and-the-legacy-of-5-indians-3yha0LldYUaH7smRsrks8A/.

the Cherokee Nation and the way that they somehow kept tribal contact with every Cherokee reaching the world over in the early 1900s. Never is brought up the topic or idea that people could have just as easily been lying for their other family members still abroad leading to Cherokee Heritage being proclaimed in Europe as I alluded to earlier. Who is to say that these opportunistic white men who paid to have their family added to the rolls, through shifty lawyers and backroom deals, didn't just also pay for other relatives who may have been still living in the Old Worlds of Europe too, making claims to heritage for land holdings as well? Who is to say that these families were not just ensuring their relatives had lands to come to out in the American West upon arrival to the new world?

The thing that should also be noted is that there were large groups of Cherokee, such as the about 1,000 Cherokees in Tennessee and North Carolina that escaped the roundup for the Trail of Tears, which did hide out in the mountains to avoid being removed for over 30 years. They gained recognition as a distinct group of peoples in 1866 and established their tribal government in 1868 in Cherokee, North Carolina. These Indians that escaped by hiding in the hills are now a part of what is known as the Eastern Band of Cherokee Indians.[176] So there is irrefutable proof that groups of Cherokee not only could, but did, move as family groups still governed by their traditions, linked through their shared culture and language, to hide out in the hills from the racism, discrimination, and the oppression that they had felt in their past homelands.

Let us look at just how the current logic of the Cherokee Nation is flawed. As discussed earlier other elements of Cherokee culture kept the historical splits within the tribe continuous throughout the times. While some Cherokee, like Emmet Starr, did travel to visit with the Western Cherokee, the accounts of the Western Cherokee's history only really talk of the peoples that

---

[176] "Cherokee." *NCpedia*, www.ncpedia.org/cherokee/trailoftears.

would eventually go on to the lands in Oklahoma. However, that does not mean that every Western Cherokee person removed further west. There are families of Cherokee that did escape from the Trail of Tears that do disappear, and never returned to the mass tribal body. These families often lived out their lives in the Ozark mountains. Factors like the Cherokee Blood Law, intertribal racism, Tribal Politics, and other past events caused groups to separate from the main body with a portion of these people never returning; while some Cherokee groups did return to the mass group, such as the group of Eastern Cherokees that moved to Stilwell, Oklahoma in the 1870s, that doesn't mean that all groups do so. To prove my case in point, we can look to the Southern Cherokee people who left Indian Territory settling back into the Ozark mountains of Arkansas & Missouri after the group was disenfranchised from the main body politic after the Civil War. Splits happen within groups but to say that these individual Cherokees, who either escaped the Trail of Tears, or chose to stay in Arkansas and Missouri not wanting to conform to the new rules established by these eastern immigrant Cherokees relocating to Indian Territory, did not relocate but also could not have lived in smaller groups that came together at a later time in the Ozarks is insane as Inter displaced peoples such as the Jewish populations of Europe and Russia are seen, during the same time period, grouping together in new settlements in a piecemeal fashion in places of past inhabitants of their ancestors.

For instance, In the first Aliyah immigrants came into the lands of what would later become Israel because of the connection they felt to the land of their ancestors rather than having a sense of shared location of origin, sharing the same admixture in terms of European decent, or even a shared language. These Jewish settlements were built up by families or people, traveling as individuals and small groups, from Europe and Russia only reuniting into a mass identifiable group of peoples once they were in the homelands of their ancestors. The settlements produced were built up one person at a time with only some of the new settlers coming in an organized fashion or as mass groups from Europe to populate the areas. Moving on in time we can compare the post holocaust population of Jewish peoples, also known as survivors, and their experiences in America and see some correlations between the lifestyles of survivors and that of the post Trail of Tears Cherokee population living under Jim Crow. The research shows that, "the survivors who came to America after the war were generally between the ages of 15 and 35. A lot of the people interviewed were not in the camps, they were in hiding. Our definition of a survivor includes people who were in labor camps, people who hid, people who passed as gentiles, people who were in ghettoes, and people who went to Siberia. The criteria were people who had been dislocated during the war starting with 1939." With some researchers arguing that, "being in a situation of hiding was in some ways even worse than being in the camps because in the camps one developed a certain level of expectations, but those in hiding every day never knew when they went to sleep that they might be awakened, apprehended and killed".[177] Just as the Holocaust had an effect on the survivors the disenfranchised Natives in the Ozarks lived in the same type of fear as a result of living in hiding for so many years. Often when talking with older members of the Southern Cherokee one hears stories of their experiences as children, during the 1950s until more recent years, stories that tell of their parents and grandparents hiding them from any unknown visitors who came by their homes. Darla Mathews, a member of the Southern Cherokee, once told me that before her mother was willing to enroll in the tribe, she had to be promised that she would not be made to move to Oklahoma, as this was a real fear for her. I was explained that her reaction to the idea of enrolling on paper was like one that a person would have if they were being told to break the law in some way. This is because, for her, and the others that cling to this worldview of fear, it goes against their

---

[177] "Don't Look Back: Holocaust Survivors in the U.S." Jerusalem Center for Public Affairs, jcpa.org/article/dont-look-back-holocaust-survivors-in-the-u-s/.

long-held family tradition of rejecting rolls that have been followed in the past.

The movements of other oppressed populations disprove the current theory held by the already Federally Recognized tribes that even if there were deserters of the trail, which there undeniably were, they could not have, in any practical manor, hid out in the hills and govern themselves and produced new tribal bodies with unique practices in the current day. These claims made by the recognized groups spit in the face of our shared heritage as it is known that the Cherokees were a confederacy of multiple smaller tribal bodies united by culture, lands, and language. Before the white rule of the American continents, one did not have to be of blood to be recognized by the peoples in the Cherokee Nation of Old, and in lesser cases, during the reorganization of the Chickamauga peoples. This statement is proven in the historical records, with individuals of Anglo decent having Cherokee Citizenship link through their culture and not blood, such as Chief William Holland Thomas.[178]

In the late 1700s to the early 1800s, before the removals, a lot of Cherokees had intermixed and had an amalgamation of Irish and Cherokee culture or Cherokee and another tribe such as the many Nassayn groups, the Delaware, the Chickasaw, and the Choctaw to name a few, creating their own new brands of Cherokee heritage and culture, that has been covered up until this point, that could be found throughout the families within these linked communities. Seeing as the Ozarks has a historical record of pockets of inter-tribal groups such as these it is quite possible, I would dare to even say probable, that these new populations did not see the tribal remnants that could now be found in Oklahoma after the Removal Period as a Nation that they still felt a part of in anyway by the mid-1850s, with no change in this opinion until modern times. This is because white factions had invaded the Dawes Rolls and the Cherokee tribe in Oklahoma

---

[178] "Cherokee." *NCpedia*, www.ncpedia.org/cherokee/trailoftears.

creating permanent splits between the people. However, at their core these groups self-identified as Native Americans, more specifically Cherokees, and are still present in the Ozarks today. Although their practices may have adapted, and appropriated, from their other cultures in the process, they are at their core still Native American Groups. Regardless to the Tribal body, the only way to move forward as indigenous peoples is to act as a united front on the political stage, as we should all stand together and recognize that we have barely survived through 500 years of oppression as separate groups, and the only way to survive for another 500 years is to support each other in the fight for our voices to be heard by the masses once more.

APPENDIX A:

Guy Smith's Blackfoot Chickamauga/Southern Cherokee Family

My Great Grandfather on my dad's father's side, James F. Smith, and the husband of Arvella Nichols. James was Chickamauga Cherokee, descendent from Old Settlers/Southern Cherokee who settled in the Arkansas River Valley; nicknamed "Corn Smith", he passed away in Oklahoma where he lived and worked as a farmer/moonshiner most his life.

Arvella Nichols was a Blackfoot Chickamauga Cherokee from the Mountain Community in the Arkansas River Valley.

 Guy Smith

Arvella's brother Earl pictured with his wife. Earl was a Mountain Community member; he is also the one who is recorded giving an account of what life was like at "The Mountain".

My Great Grandfather James' sister Matilda Shelton née Smith, and her husband Vergil Shelton, Chickamauga Cherokees from Ozark, Arkansas, in the Arkansas River Valley.

*My Great Grandmother Arvella Smith née Nichols
photographed and my Great Grand Aunt, her sister Thelma
Davidson née Nichols, pictured standing behind here.*

*My 2nd Great Grandfather, Burl Nichols, with wife,
my 2nd Great Grandmother, Naomie Moore,
and their daughters. Burl and Naomie are the parents
to my Great Grandmother Arvella. They are Blackfoot
Chickamauga Cherokees from "The Mountain"
Community in the Arkansas River Valley.*

Burl and Naomie with Grandchildren,
Fort Smith, Arkansas, about 1957

*My 3rd great grandmother on my father's mother's side is
Emma Moore, maiden name Fletcher, she is pictured here
with her children and husband Andrew Moore.
The Moore family was a Blackfoot Chickamauga
Cherokee family who took up residence on Crowley's Ridge
and in the swamplands of the Boot-heel of Missouri.*

Emma pictured on far left. Family Oral history claims Emma was born in Tennessee before her family removed to the Foothills of the Ozark Highlands on Crowley's Ridge in the Mississippi Alluvial River Plains to escape "the whites" who were becoming increasingly violent to our peoples.

*My 2ⁿᵈ Great Grandfather, Emma Fletcher's son
Traymon Moore and his wife, my 2ⁿᵈ Great Grandmother,
Amelia Greer. They are Blackfoot Chickamauga
Cherokees from Northeastern Arkansas*

Traymon with brothers and their respective wives.

Traymon and Amelia Moore

*Traymon's younger brother Thomas Moore before
shipping off to fight in WWII*

*Emma Fletcher's sons photographed. The names appear in order from
left to right: Dodson Joshua Moore, Thomas Ewuen Moore, Virgil
Featherston Moore, Traymon Moore, Talmadge Eugene Moore*

Thomas Moore

Virgil, Thomas, Earl Moore at their father's,
Andrew Moore, Grave

Caruthersville, Pemiscot County, Missouri

*Traymon's siblings Virgil Featherston and Thomas Ewuen Moore
at grave their mother of Emma Fletcher.*

*My Paternal Great Grandmother on my dad's mothers' side,
Lula Grokett, a Choctaw, and Chickasaw whose son, Lloyd,
married into the Blackfoot Chickamauga Cherokee Moore Family*

Lloyd Grokett, my maternal great-grandfather, he was Choctaw and Chickasaw Indian from Oklahoma and he married into the Chickamauga Cherokee in Arkansas, before shipping out to fight in the Korean War.

APPENDIX B:

Other Pictures & Maps Referenced

Chick Allen, circa 1964, is pictured wearing a black hat on the far Right, preforming at the opening of Silver Dollar City, an Americana styled Theme Park that is located between Branson and Branson West on the Indian Point peninsula of Table Rock Lake, Missouri.[179]

179 Crabtree, Richard. Love My Ozarks History, 13 Mar. 2019, www.facebook. com/search/top/?q=chick allen&epa=SEARCH_BOX.

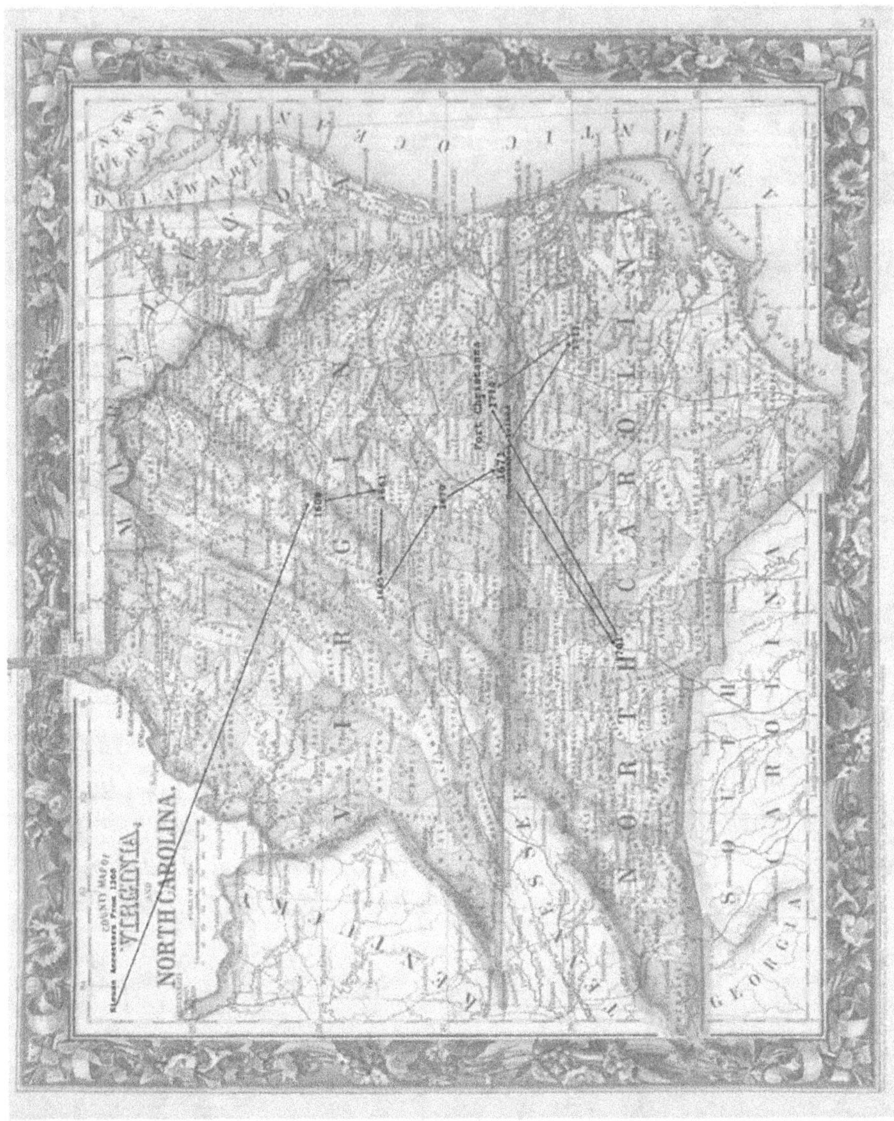

Map of the Sightings of the Nassayn/Saponi peoples prior to their movement into Fort Christanna in 1714

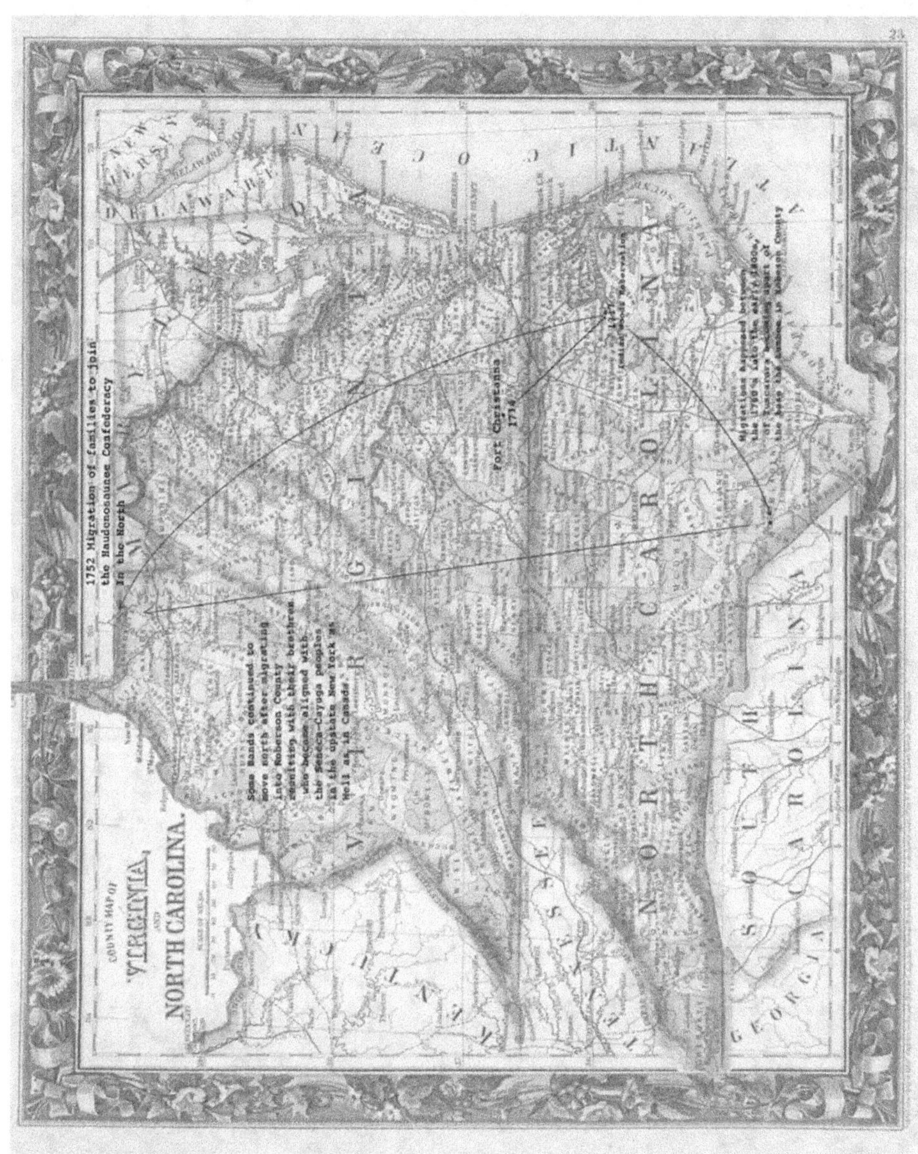

Map of the Tuscarora Bands out of Fort Christanna

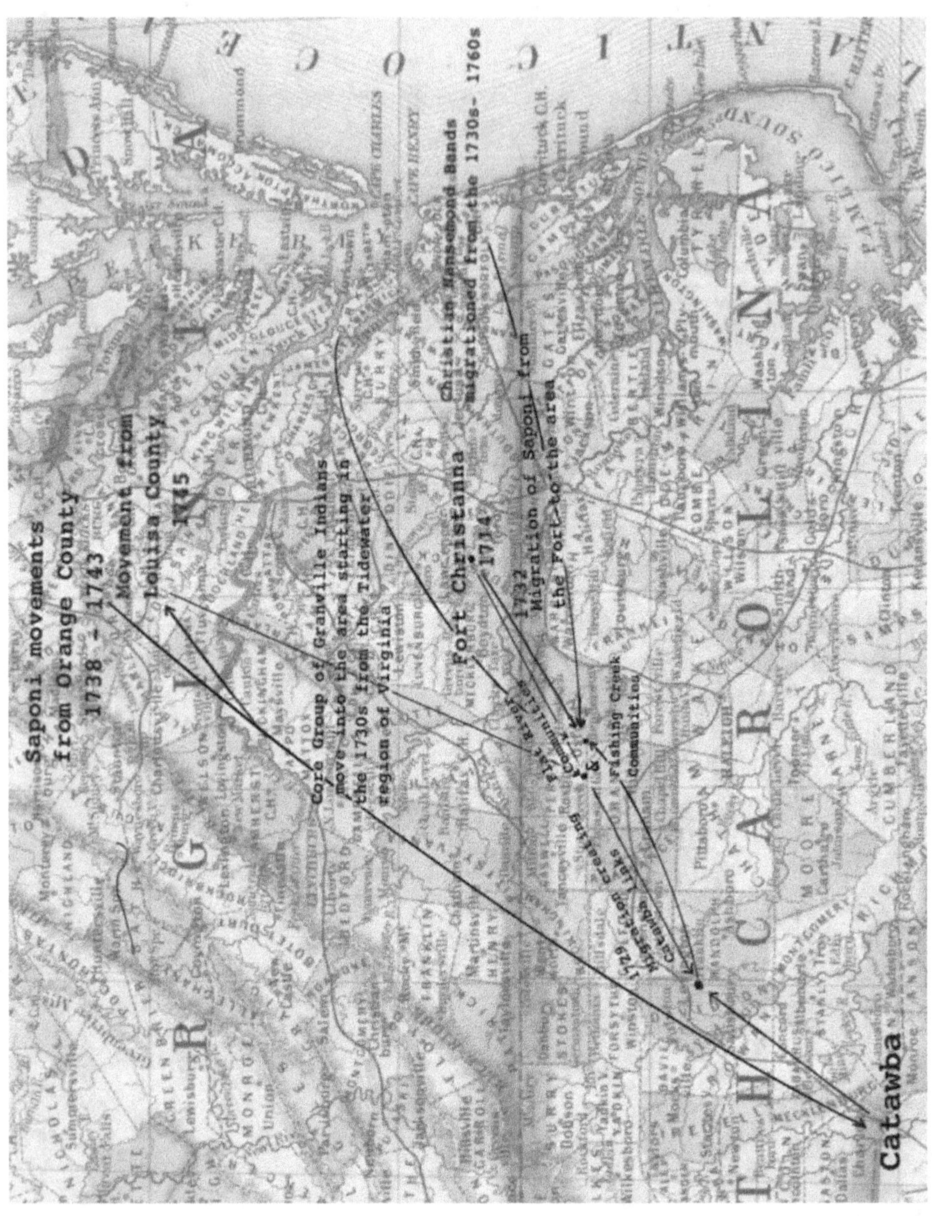

Map of the settlement of the Fishing Creek and
Flat River Indian Communities

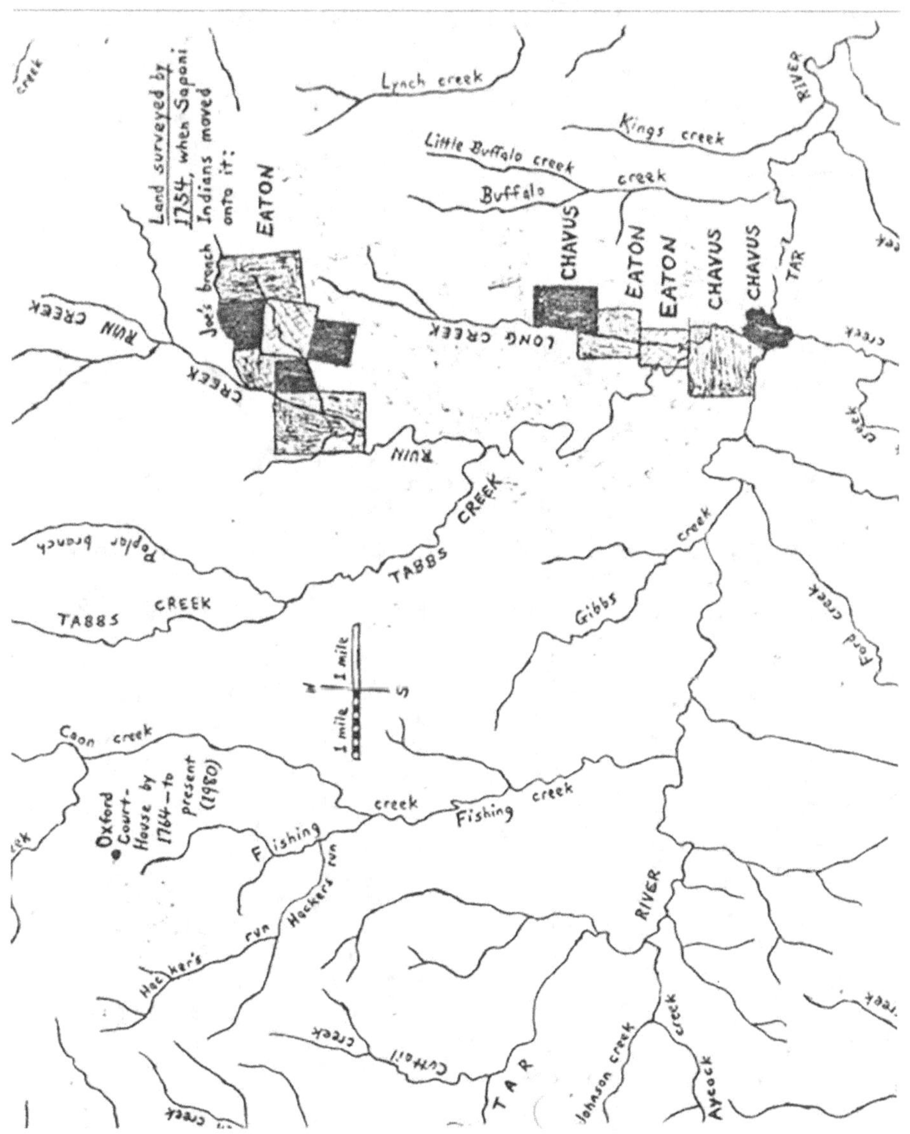

This Map shows the plots of the original Saponi and allied landowners in the 1750s[180]

---

[180] Lucas, Kianga. "Yearly Archives: 2015." *Native American Roots*, nativeamerican roots.wordpress.com/2015/page/3/.

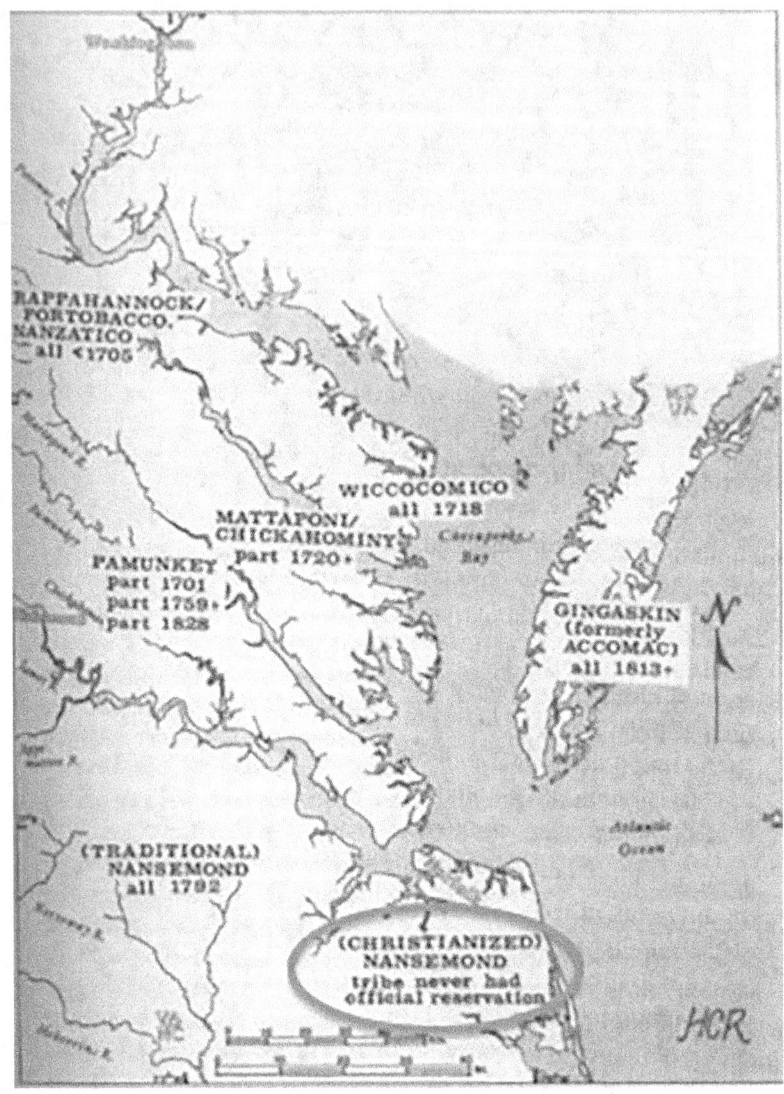

A map of the Virginia tribes that notes the lack of
Reservation for the Christianized group of Nansemond.[181]

---

[181] "Nansemond Map." Native American Roots, nativeamericanroots.files.
wordpress.com/2015/05/christianized-nansemond-map1.jpg.

Alonzo Bass (1859-1941).
Son of William Bass and Sarah Evans.[182]

---

[182] Lucas, Kianga. "Yearly Archives: 2015." *Native American Roots,* nativeamer-icanroots.wordpress.com/2015/page/3/.

Augustus Bass *sitting on the far left with other members of his family in Norfolk County, VA. Augustus Bass is a descendant of William Bass Jr (1676-1761), whose family remained in Norfolk, Virginia.*[183]

---

[183] Ibid.

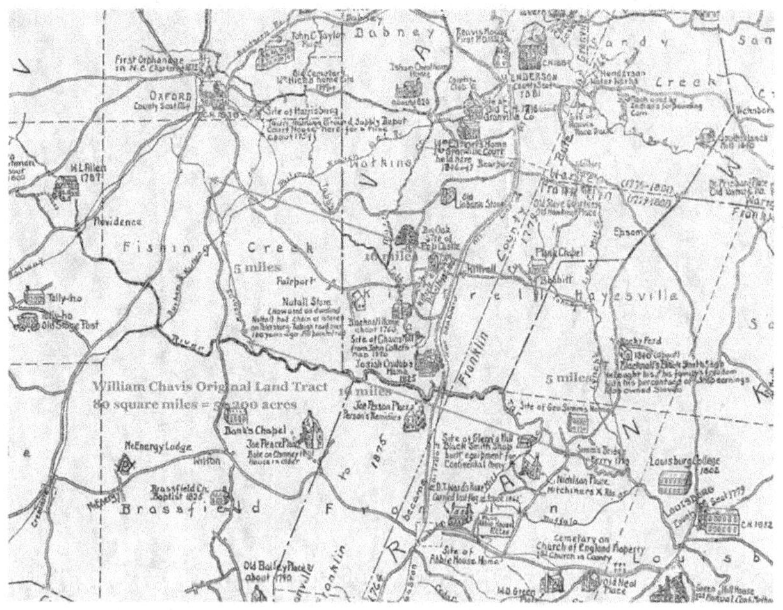

*This map shows what was the original land tract held
by the Chavis family that covered 80 square miles,
or 51,200 acres of land*[184]

[184] Lucas, Kianga. "Defining the Boundaries of the Tuscarora 'Indian Woods' Reservation in Bertie County." *Native American Roots*, 10 July 2015, nativeamericanroots.wordpress.com/2015/07/10/defining-the-boundaries-of-the-tuscarora-indian-woods-reservation-in-bertie-county/?blogsub=confirming#subscribe-blog.

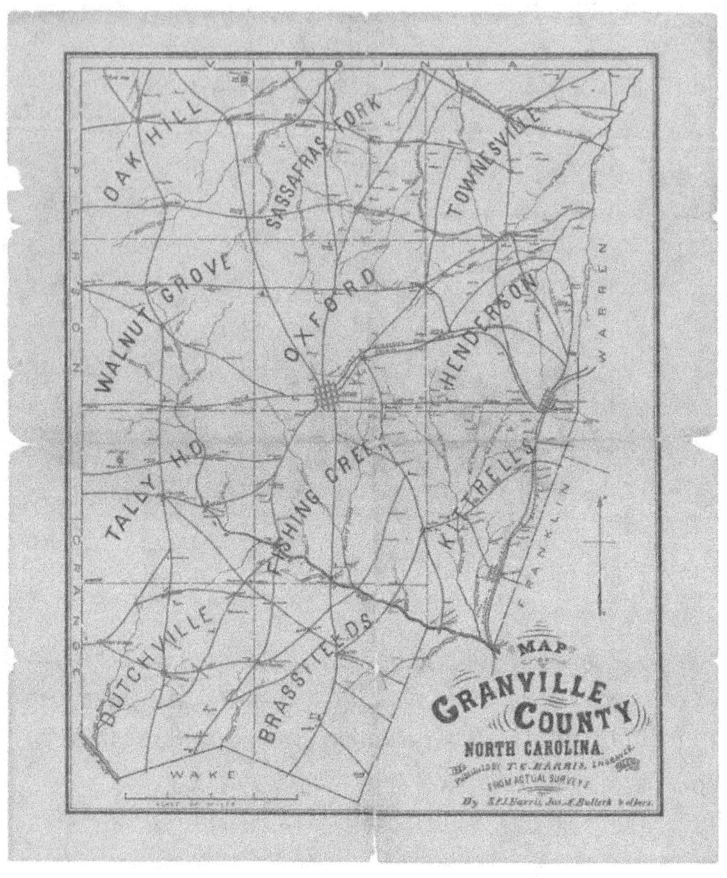

Old map of the Fishing Creek in relation to other locations[185]

---

[185] Lucas, Kianga. "Yearly Archives: 2015." *Native American Roots,* nativeamericanroots.wordpress.com/2015/page/3/.

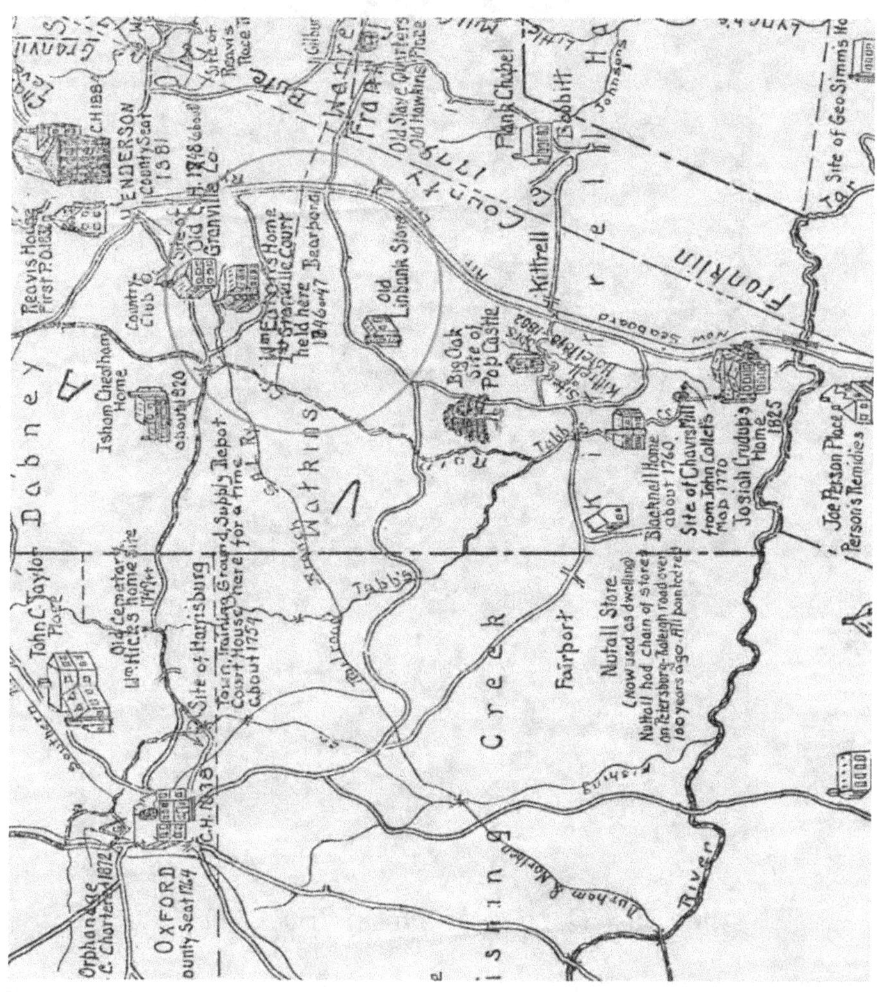

Col. William Eaton's home shown in a historical map of Granville County.[186]

---

[186] Ibid.

Joel Bass *Occaneechi-Saponi Tribal Chief*[187]

---

[187] Ibid.

Adeline Jane Howell (1858 – after 1900).
Daughter of Alexander "Doc" Howell and Betsy Ann Anderson.
She lived most of her life in the Fishing Creek township in
Granville County leaving in her later years.[188]

---

[188] Lucas, Kianga. "Freeman Howell – Ancestor of the Native American How-
ells of Granville, Orange, Person, and Alamance Counties." *Native American
Roots,* 4 Mar. 2018,

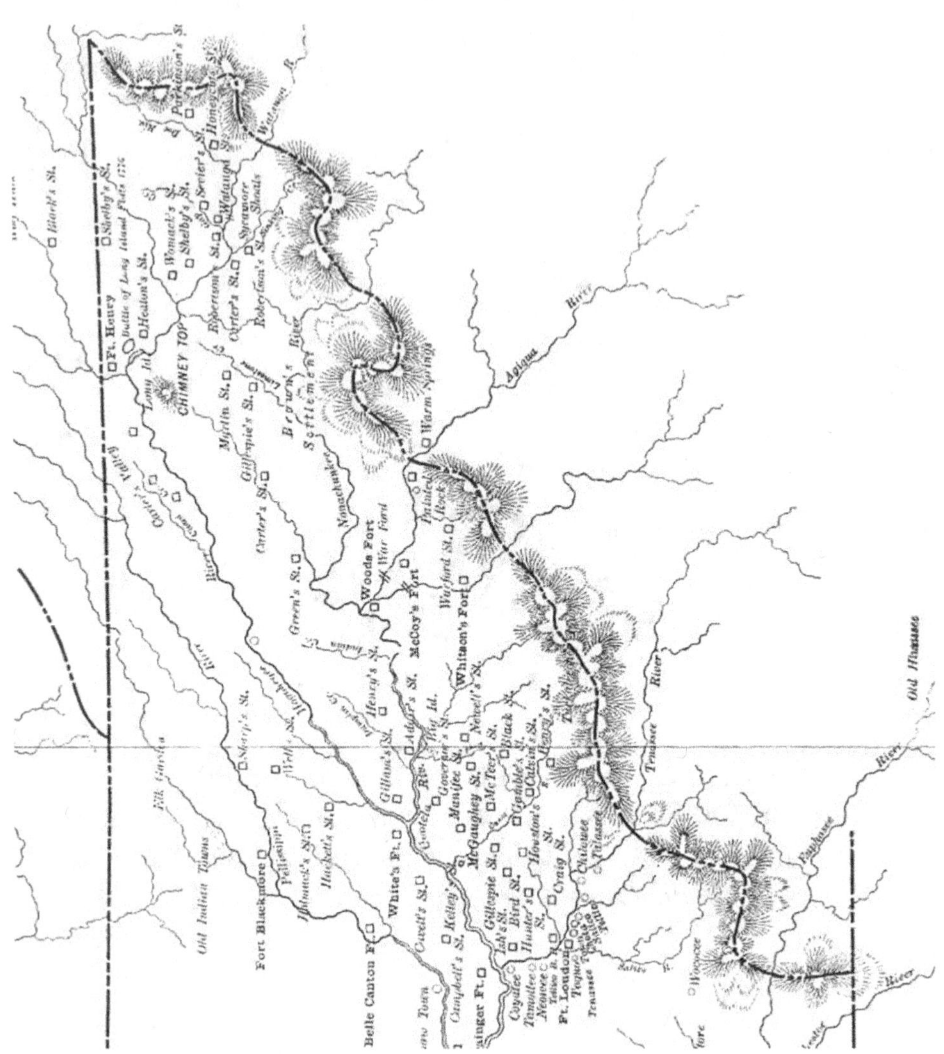

1886 Map produced by the Goodspeed Publishing Company in Nashville, Tennessee[189]

---

[189] "Goodspeed's Map of Early Tennessee." *Goodspeed's Map of Early Tennessee*, melungeon-studies.blogspot.com/2009/10/goodspeed-map-of-early-tennessee.html.

William Pettiford (1852-1932) *was the son of Susannah Brandon and William Pettiford Sr. He lived his life in Granville's Native community.*[190]

---

[190] Lucas, Kianga. "The Saponi/Monacan Indian Brandon/Branham Family of Granville County." *Native American Roots,* 2012 Nov. 2015, nativeamericanroots.wordpress.com/tag/fort-christanna/.

 Guy Smith

Grave of Tennessee Community member

*Photo A: Elderly woman who claims Cherokee heritage from the
Magoffin County group interplanting her corn with her
beans as is an indigenous practice[191]*

---

[191] Price, Edward T. "The Mixed-Blood Racial Strain of Carmel, Ohio, and
Magoffin County, Kentucky." *The Ohio Journal of Science.*, vol. 50, no. 6, Nov.
1950, pp. 281–290.

Photo B: Shows shuck beans that are strung up to dry on a porch in Tennessee. The same practice is also reported to be done by the Salyersville and Carmel Indian groups [192]

Photo C: Shows the diversity in the complexions of closely related children of the Salyersville Indian Communities[193]

---

[192] Ibid.
[193] Ibid

Photo D: A family from the Salyersville area group located in the Carmel mountains of Ohio[194]

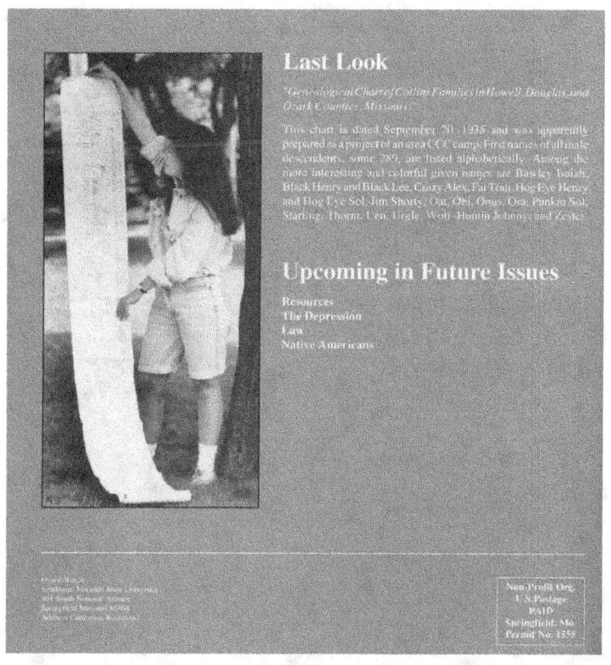

Last Look

"Genealogical Chart of Collins Families in Howell, Douglas, and Ozark Counties, Missouri"

This chart is dated September 20, 1935 and was apparently prepared as a project of an area CCC camp. First names of ultimate descendents, some 289, are listed alphabetically. Among the more interesting and colorful given names are Bawley, Isaiah, Black Henry and Black Lee, Crazy Alex, Fat Tom, Hog Eye Henry and Hog Eye Sol, Jim Shorty, Oat, Obi, Onus, Oaz, Punkin Sol, Starling, Thorm, Uen, Uvale, Wolf-Huntin Johnny, and Zester.

Upcoming in Future Issues

Resources
The Depression
Law
Native Americans

Pictured here on the back cover of Ozarks watch Magazine Is the Tribal Roll created by the CCC to track the Heads of

---

[194] Ibid.

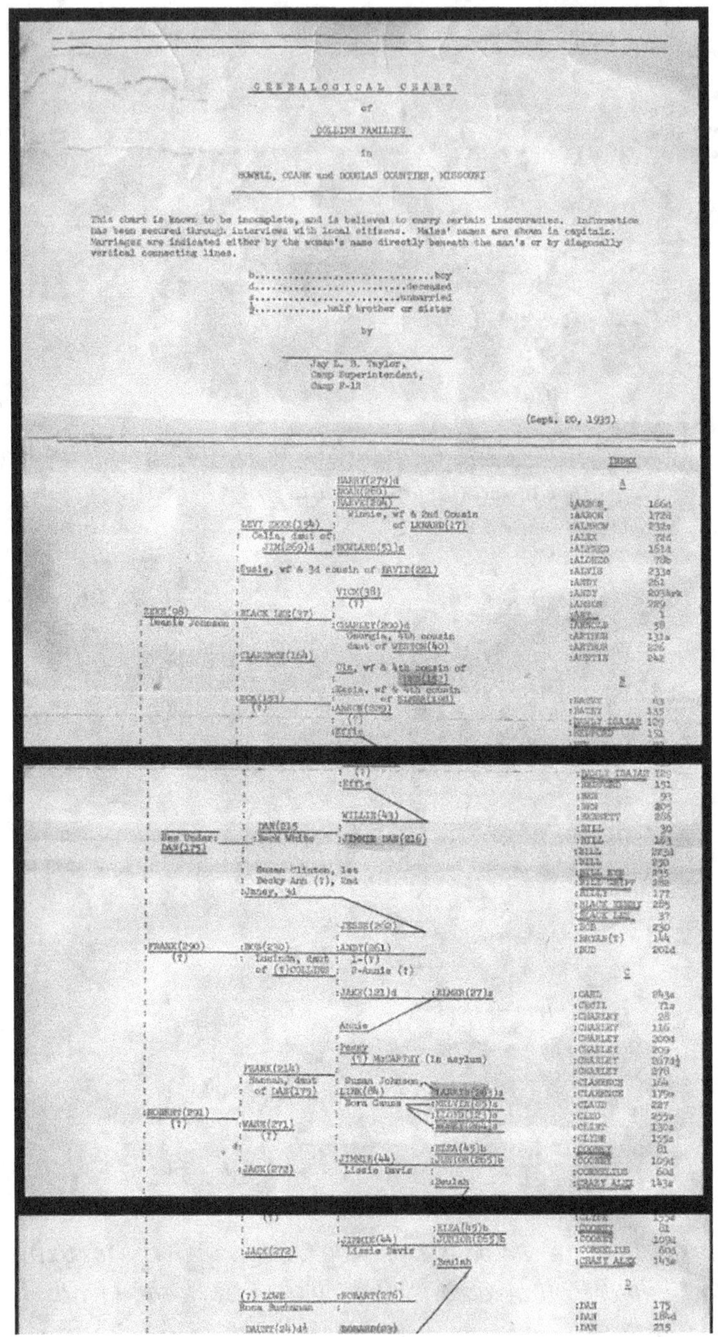

The CCC Saponi heads of house Rolls

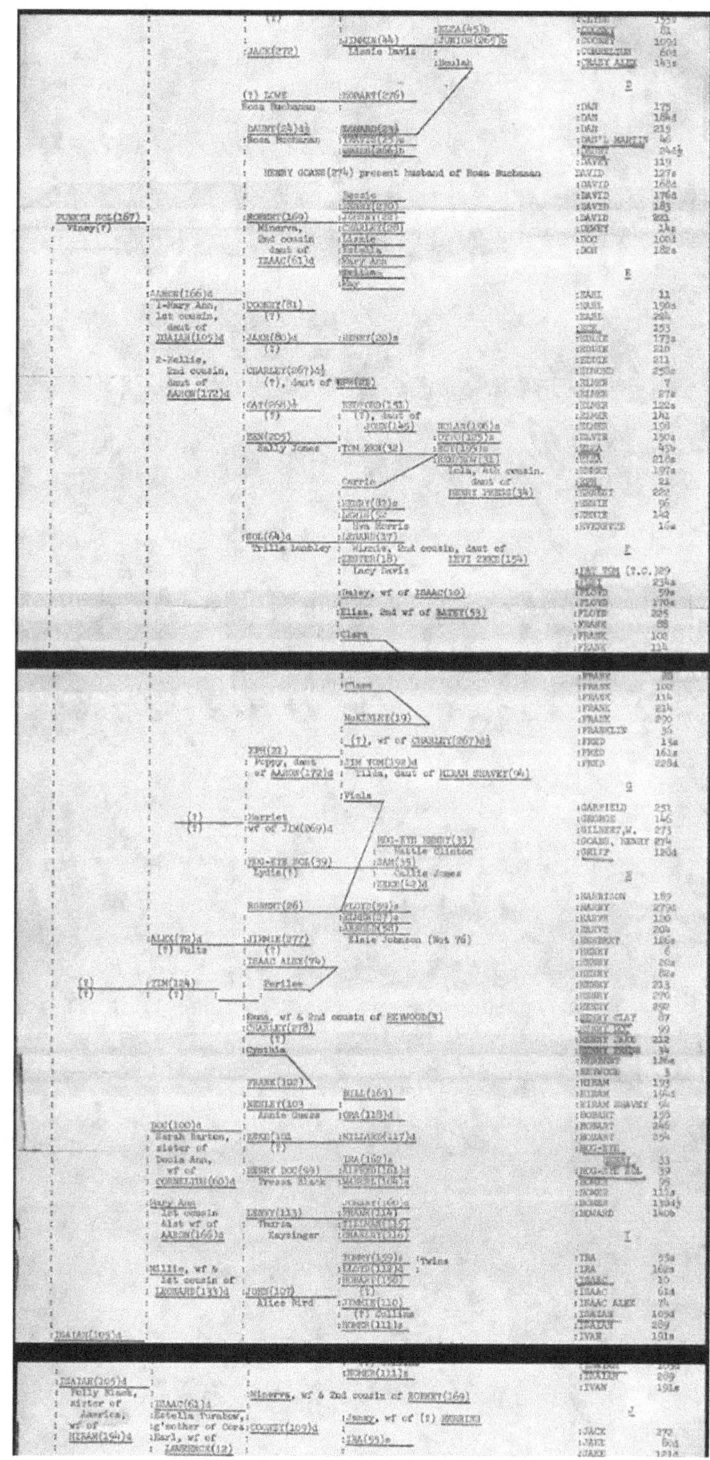

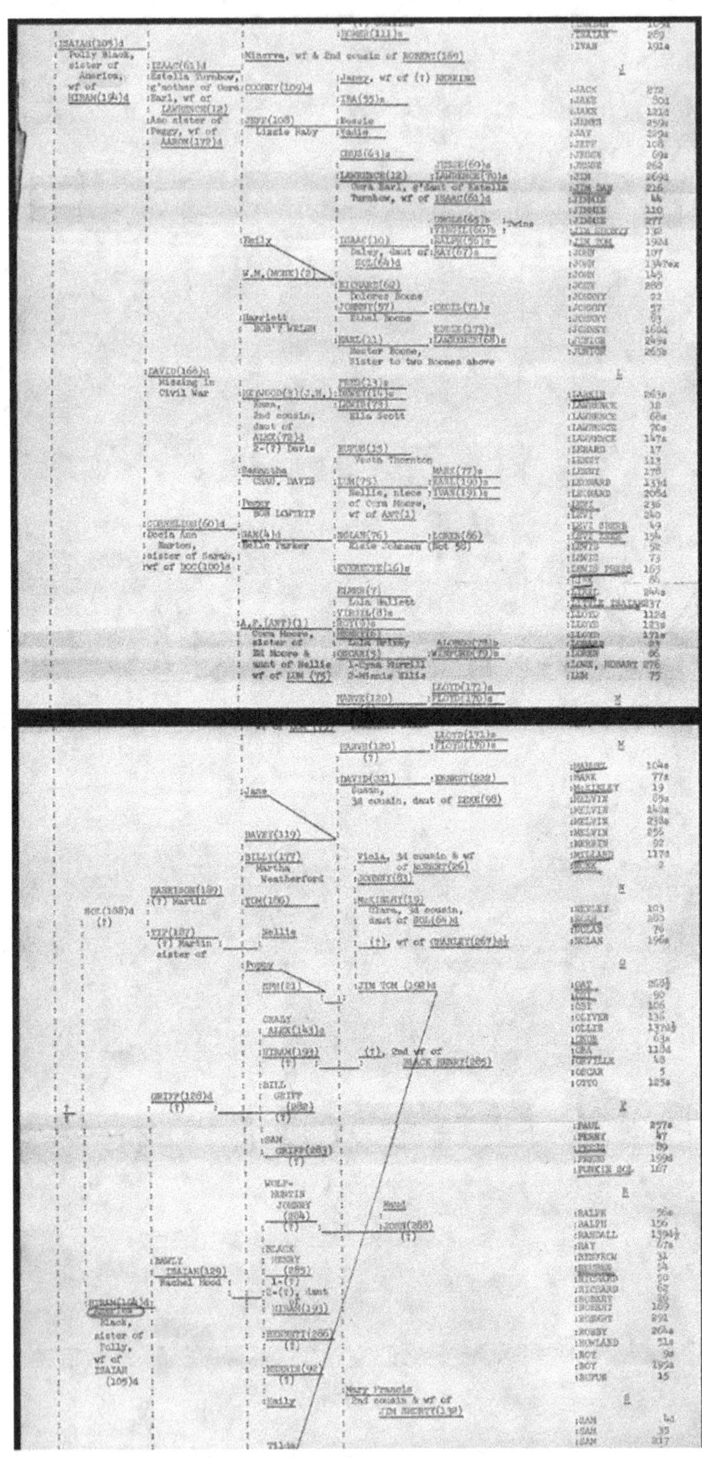

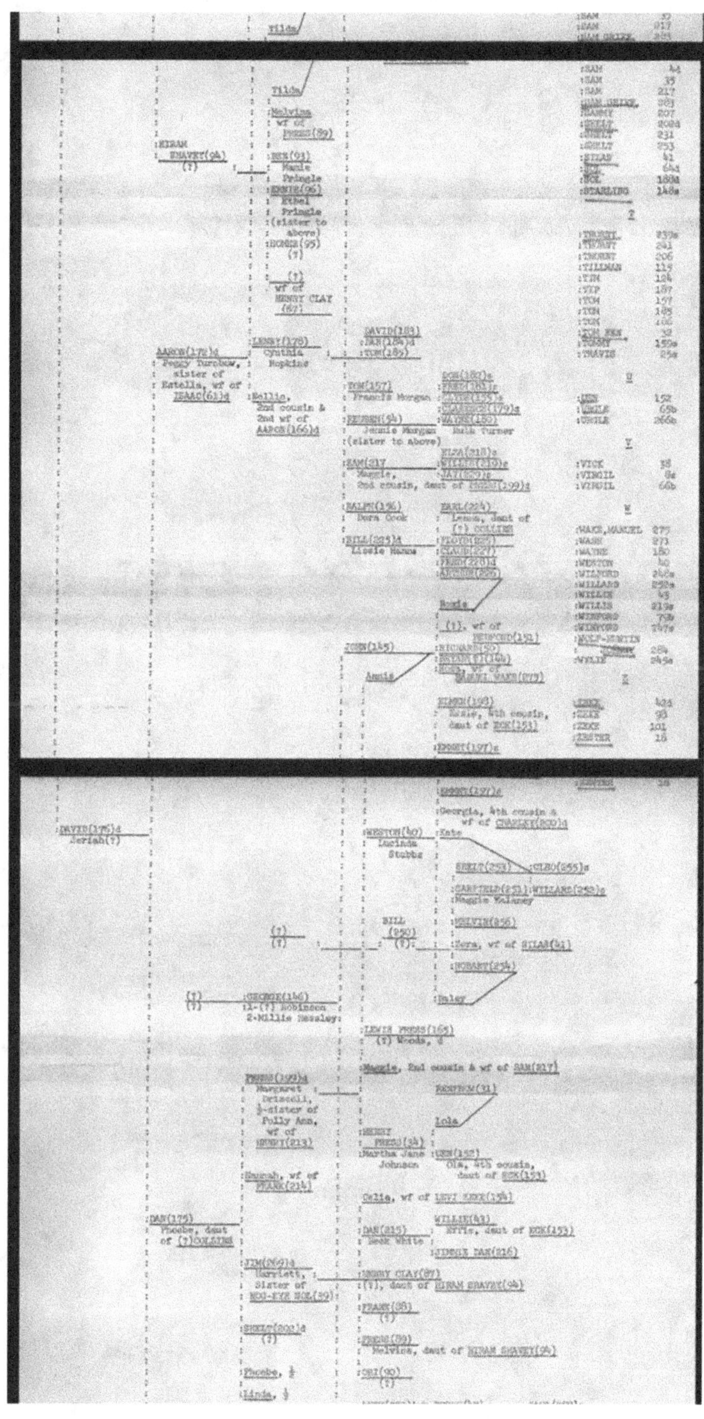

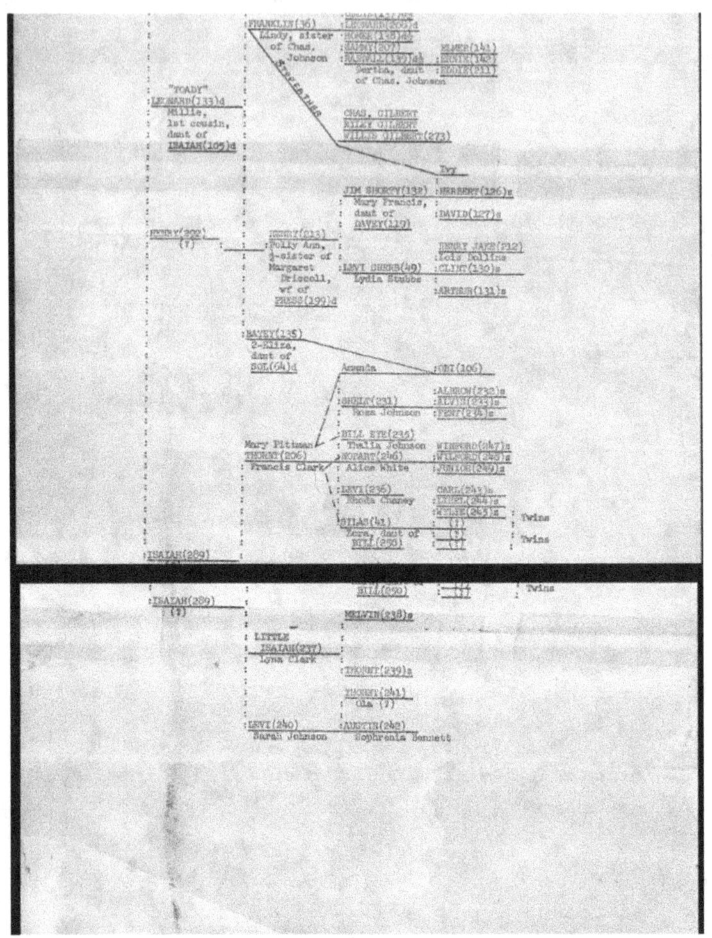

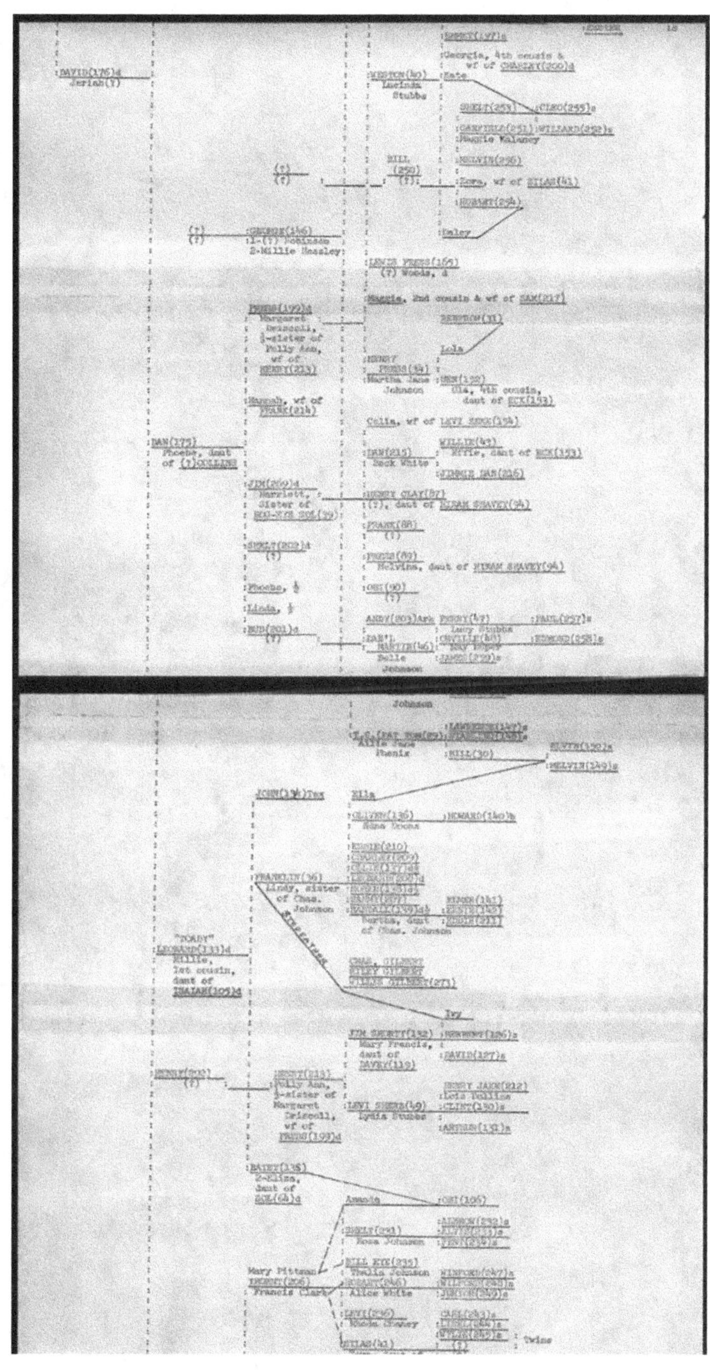

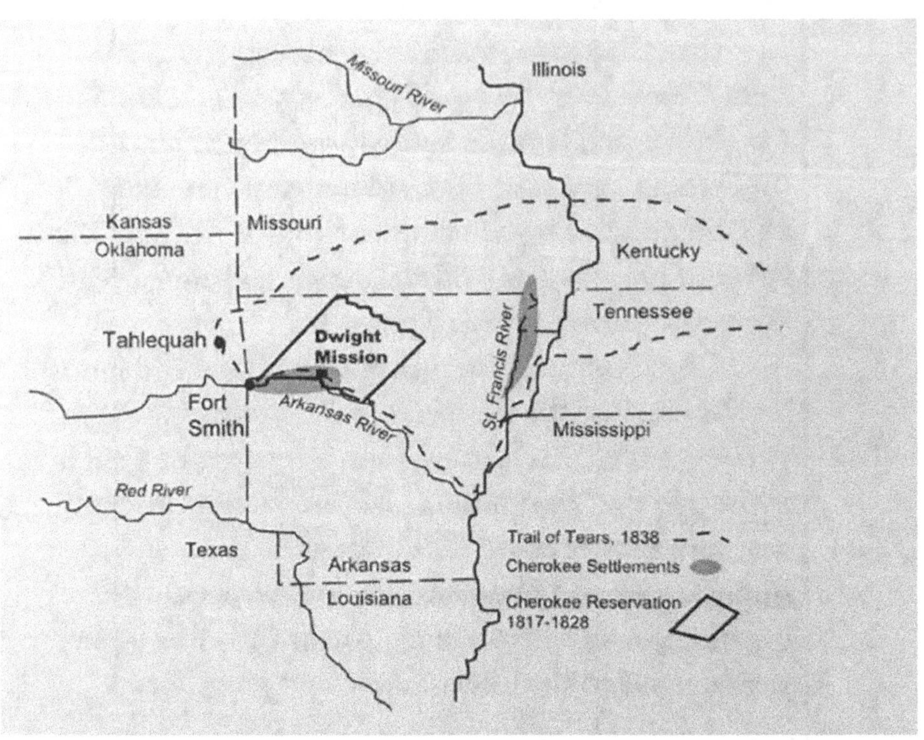

*Cherokee settlement of the Ozarks in the
first half of the 19th century*[195]

---

[195] "TOTA Conference Highlights Cherokee Old Settlers." *Cherokee Phoenix*,
www.cherokeephoenix.org/Article/index/11759.

Rev. Johnathan Wayland *A Saponi/Catawba and one of the founders of the first church in Indian Territory*[196]

---

[196] Hawkins, Vance. "Untitled." Received by Kyle Smith, *Untitled*, 29 June 2019.

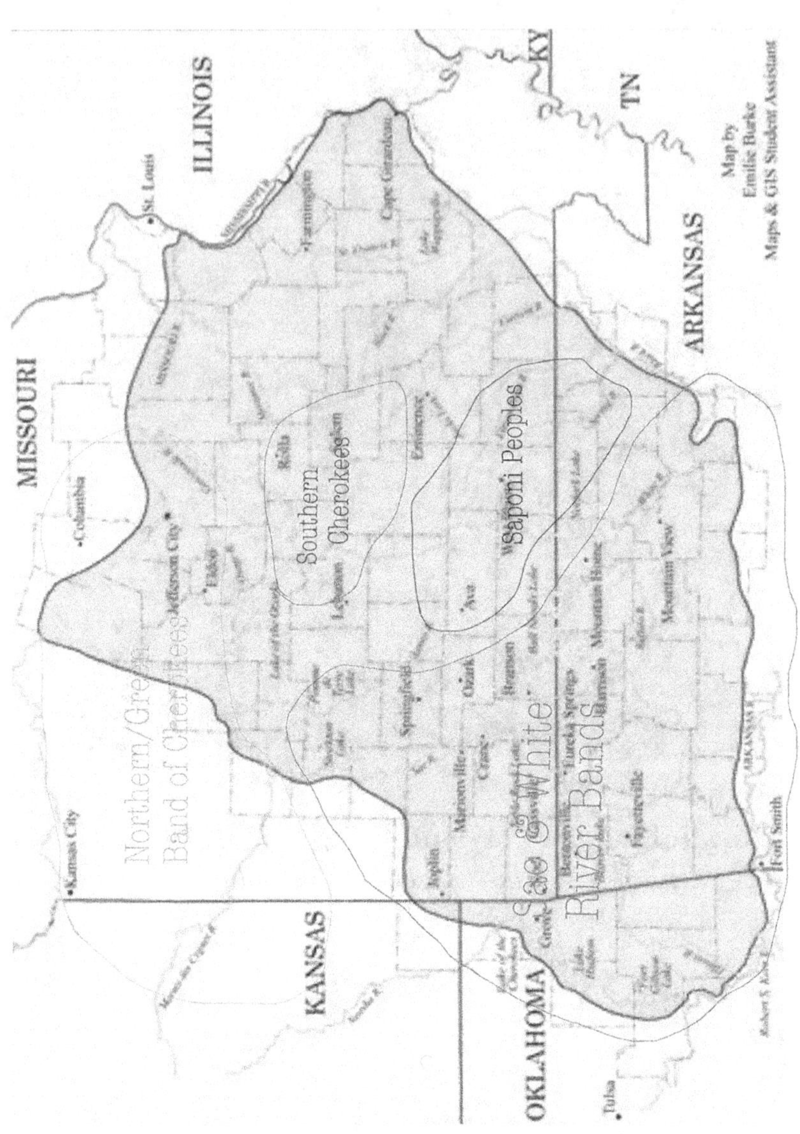

Main Areas of the primary Groups in the Ozarks
covered within this work.

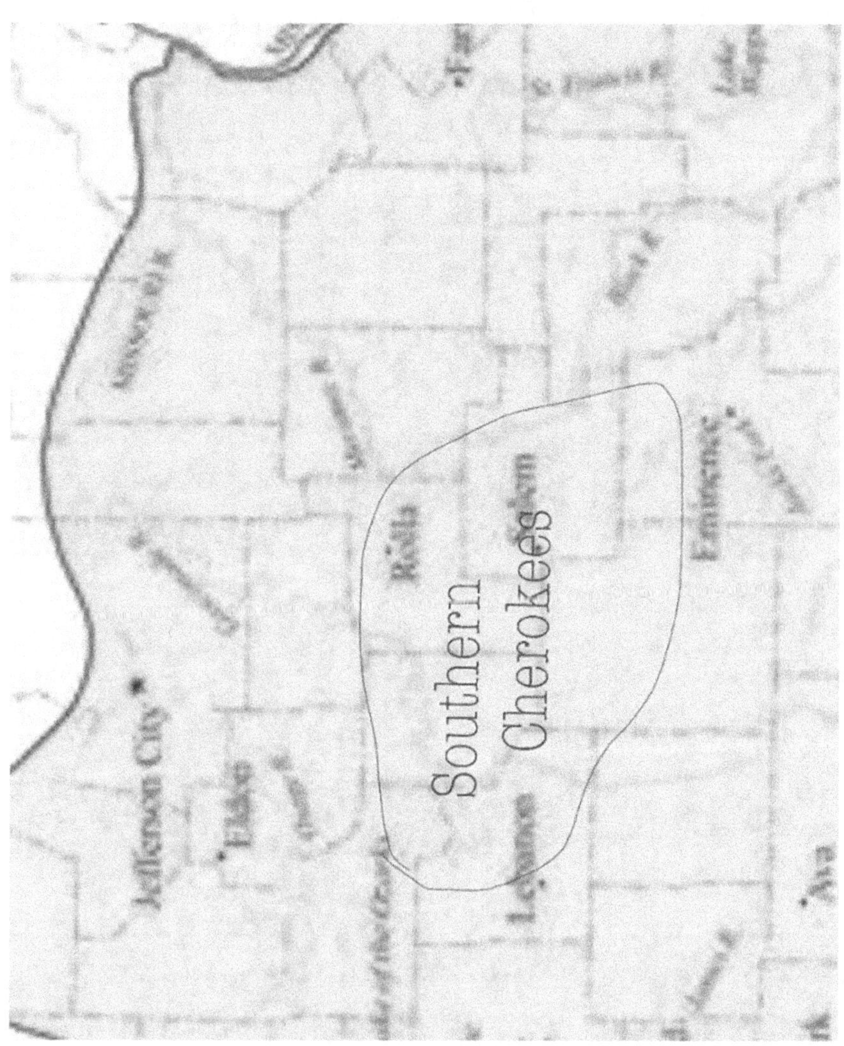

*Main Area of the Southern Cherokees Berfore going to,
and after leaving, the Cooweescoowee & Canadian Districts
in Indian Territory after the Civil War*

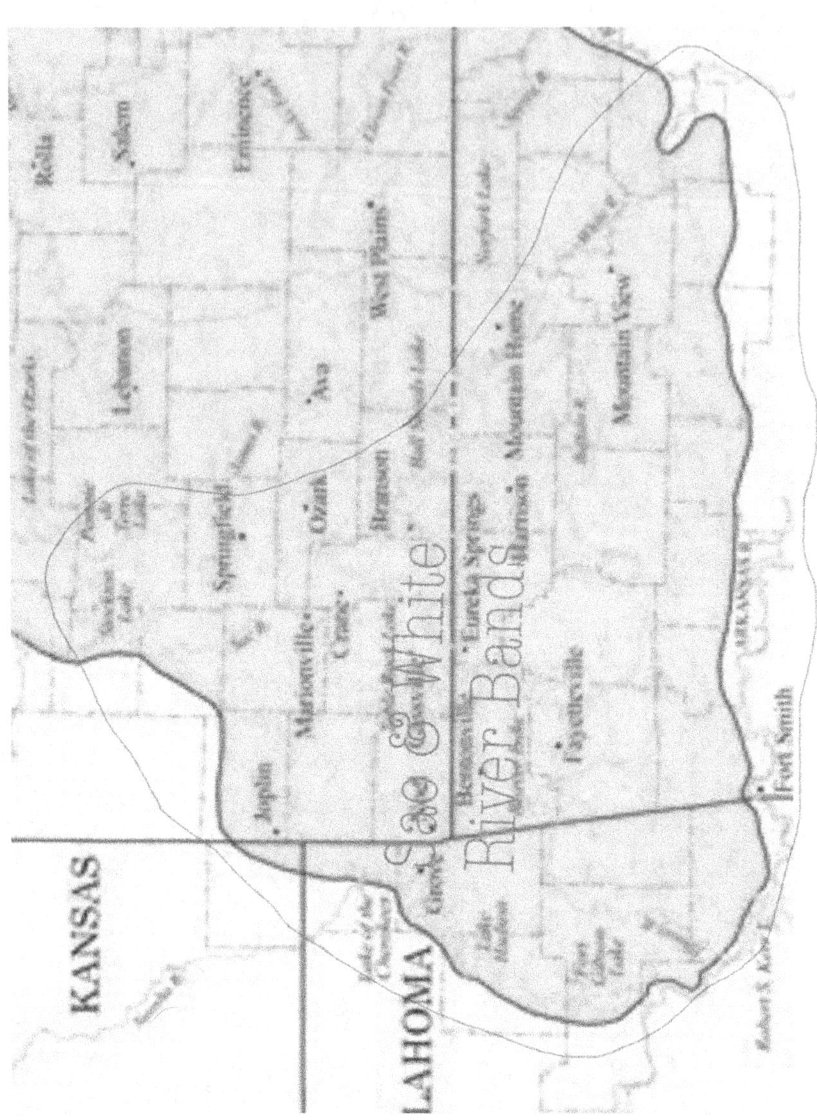

*Areas of the Sac River and White River Bands
Communities and Family Groups*

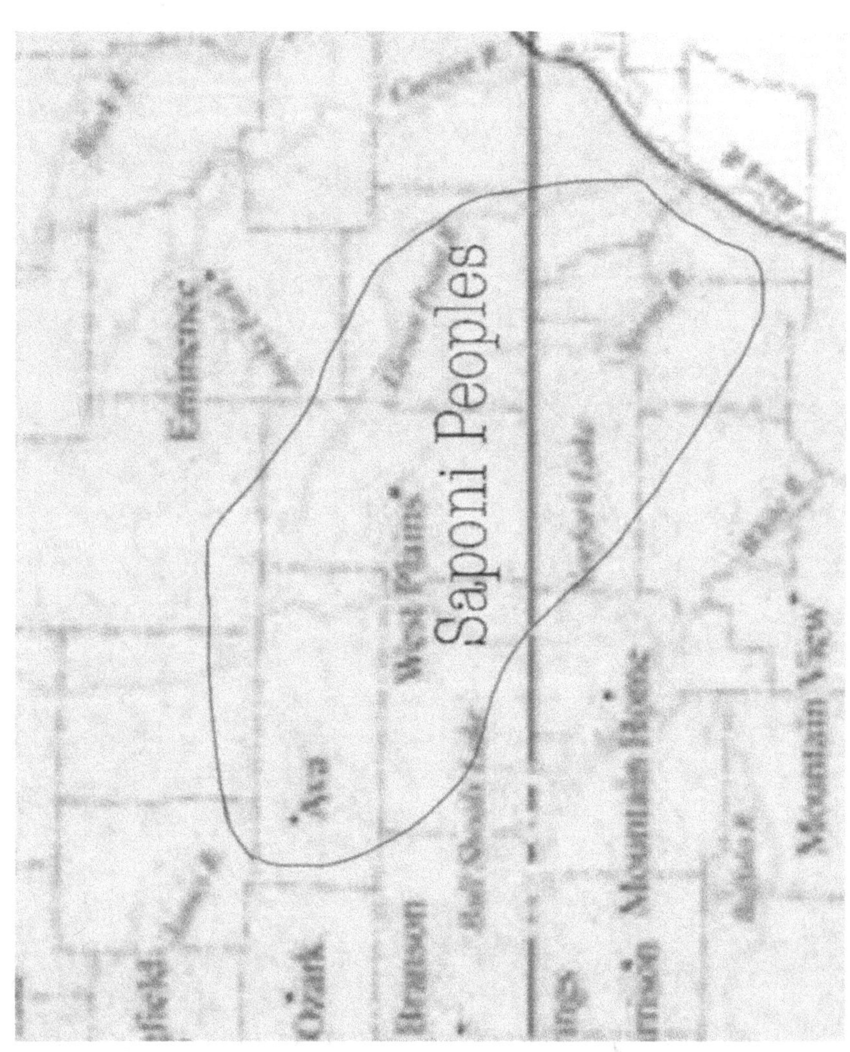

Areas of the Collins Settlements

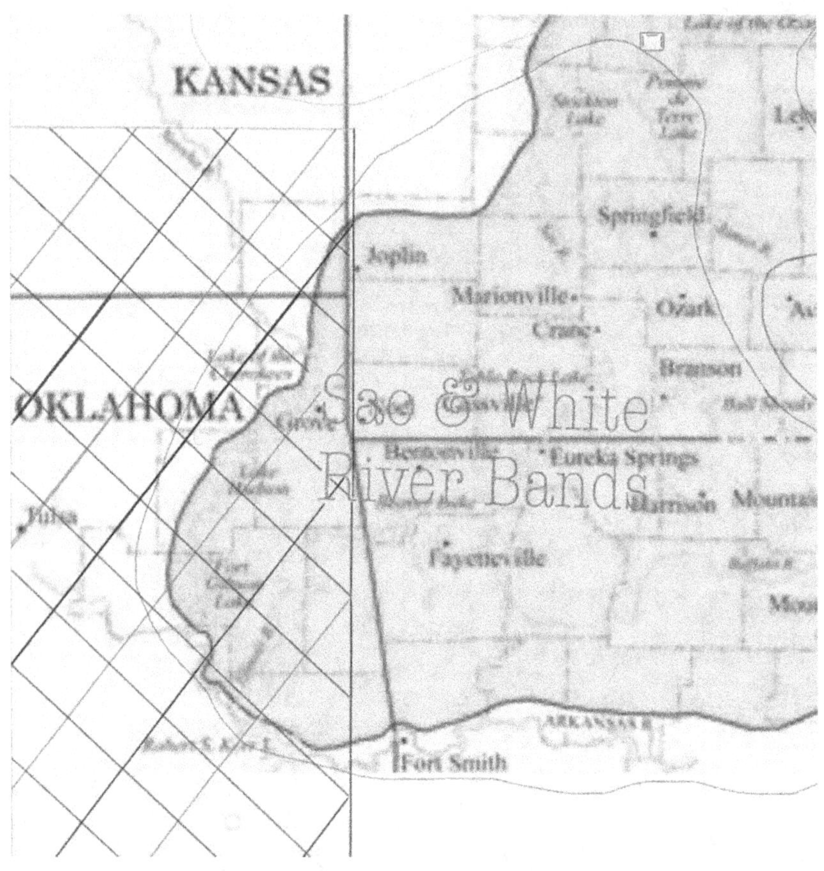

Shared Space of the Groups in Indian Territory/ Oklahoma

APPENDIX C:

Nassayn Groups Maps

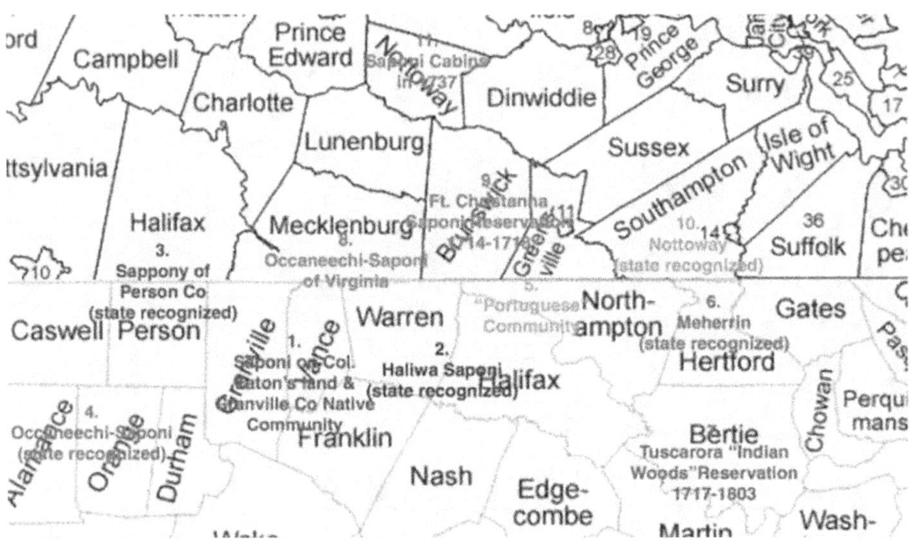

Areas of Nassayn Groups in North Carolina and Virginia[197]

---

[197] Lucas, Kianga. "Yearly Archives: 2015." *Native American Roots*, nativeamericanroots.wordpress.com/2015/page/3/..

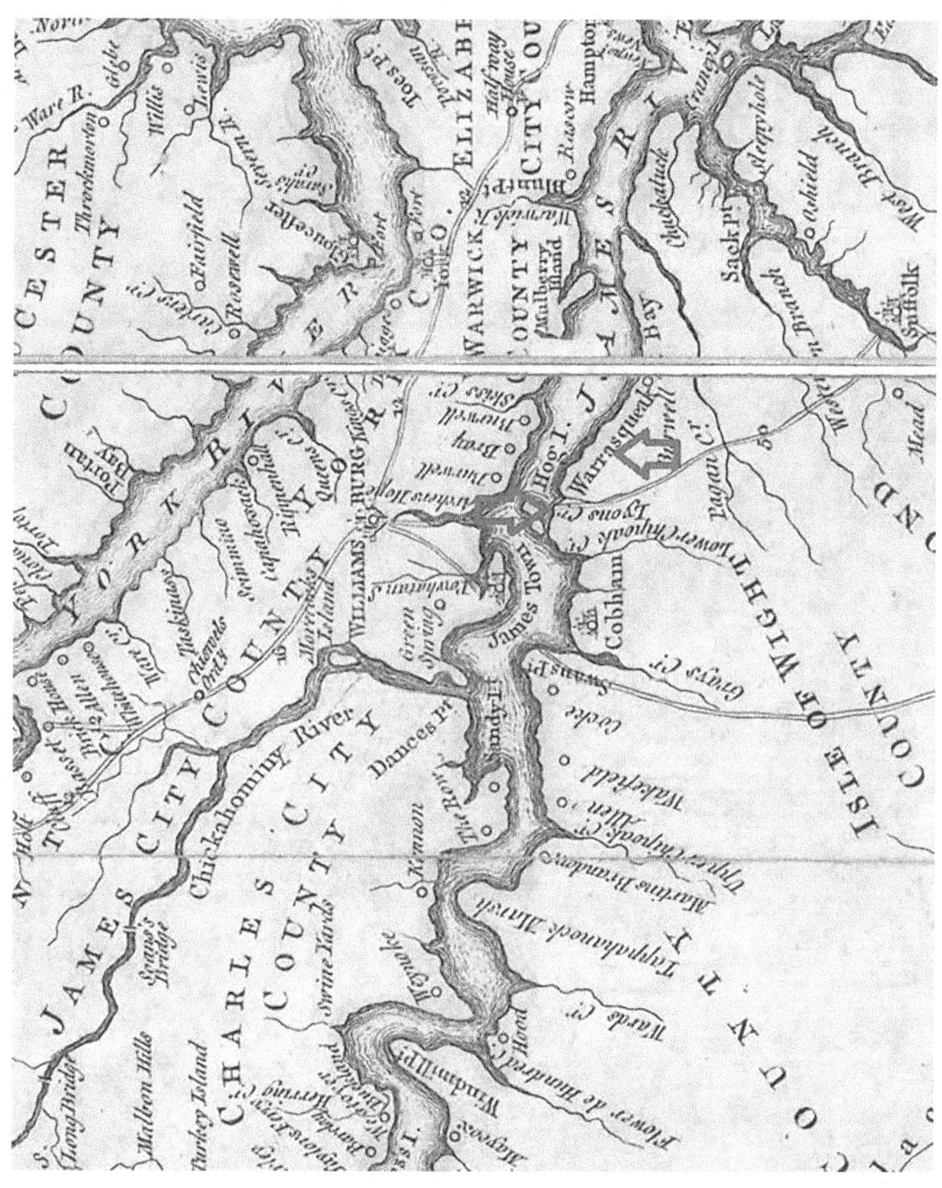

Quaker Band Map [198]

---

[198] Pezzullo, Joanne. "Warrasqueak." Received by Kyle Smith, *Warrasqueak*, 20 June 2019.

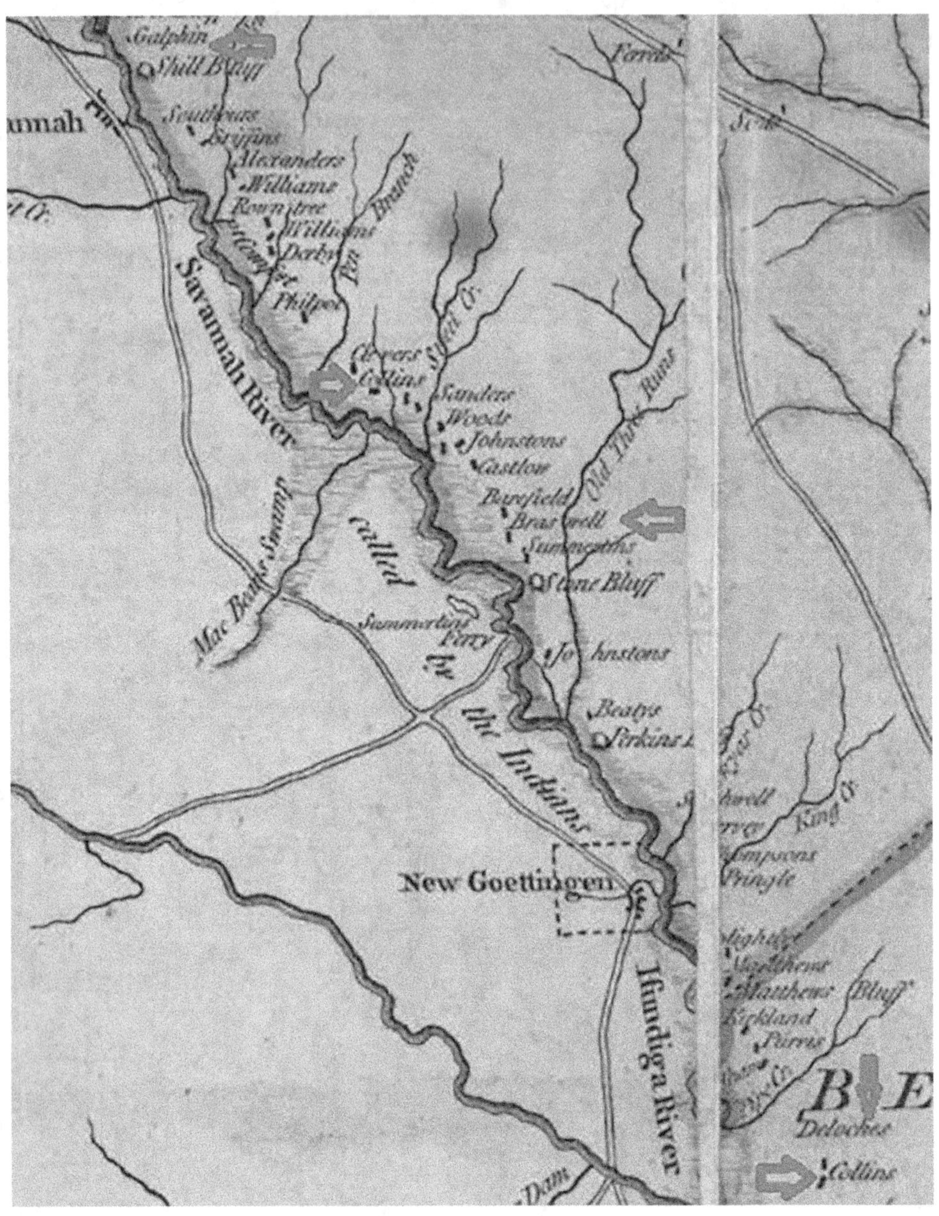

Old Three Runs Map[199]

---

[199] Ibid.

9 798435 481815